Mixed Blessings©

For my kids.

I'm nobody! Who are you?
Are you nobody, too?
Then there's a pair of us-don't tell!
They'd banish us, you know. . .

Emily Dickinson

The Early Years

Detroit is a tough town; probably always has been, but I didn't know that as a child. My earliest memories are of being loved and cared for by a mother who was always there.

She was age twenty-three, the year that I was born, and I was her second daughter. According to my Birth Certificate, that blessed event took place at Herman Kiefer Hospital, the same place that had welcomed her into the world and would later introduce her first grandchild. The date was August 14th and the year was 1949. The time was 6:23 p.m.

Mary Tramell was labeled "colored" back then as was my twenty-seven year old father, Harold Ferguson, who was also shown to be "unemployed." They weren't together at the time as is evidenced by their differing addresses. Hers was at 3605 Burns in Inkster (her father's residence) while his remains undocumented in Detroit.

According to Mother (and I grew up calling her nothing else but: for me, it was both her title and her name), she and my father had gone their separate ways when she was pregnant with me. It would take years for me to piece together why; but, as near as I can tell, this rolling-stone papa of mine had gone down to Louisiana and gotten another female pregnant. Bad as that was, I have come to believe that my mother might have endured that embarrassment had he not married the girl, shotgun wedding though it was. After all, Mother was already his first wife, common law marriage though that was. My parent's divorce was not legally finalized, however, until 1957, *In Chancery*, interestingly enough by a Third Circuit judge with the same surname of Ferguson.

Mother used to tell me that she hated living in Inkster. As far as she was concerned, it was "*country:*" isolated, too far away from the bustling of "*Black Bottom*" where she had grown up on the east side of Detroit-that enclave of everyday black folk melding with night time throngs seeking sporting entertainment, and emplaced a little too close to the city's most elite cultural institutions.

And how she loved those places: the art and historical museums, the Main Public Library, right there on Woodward Avenue. She made sure they became mainstays for my sister and me and later on for our children.

At the time she met my father, Mother had dreams of taking classes at Wayne University. He, on the other hand, had already attended Arkansas State College, and Hampton Institute, and was enrolled at the Detroit Institute of Commerce where he was President of the Business Men's Club. She was pretty, he was handsome, and they had a lot in common when they got together.

My mother's mother, Melrose, was a *fox* who loved the nightlife and having two lovely, young daughters at home was starting to cramp her style. She encouraged all three of her children, including the youngest, my Uncle Bobby, their father's namesake, to move out. So my parents simply got a place together, set up a homestead, and declared themselves husband and wife a´la Common Law. It was known, it was legal, and it was acceptable.

My sister, Anita Maria (she would hyphenate those two names later), was born October 8, 1947.

I never lived in the same household as my father which may be why he never seemed to quite take to me. We never fully bonded. I knew who he was all right, whenever he came around, which wasn't all that often. The rumor mill had it that he once claimed that I was not his child but it's doubtful anyone who knew my mother believed him. It was seemingly merely one of his ploys to get out of paying child support. But when he did show up, I yearned for his attention as much as any child who has an absentee father. But the dotage mostly went to my sister. Still, my mother always insisted he take both of us whenever he'd pick us up for an outing. *What was good for one was good for the other*, she always said.

The excursions I remember most were to a Howard Johnson's restaurant on Woodward in Highland Park where he delighted us by removing and then reinserting an upper bridge plate into his mouth. Then, there was a bar on the west side where I occasionally got to perch and twirl on one of the stools; and a couple of different houses where various Ferguson family members might be gathered for a particular occasion, and where I always felt unwanted, like I didn't belong. The only time I recall it being different was when one young cousin, James Tinsley, joined me outside for a brief chit-chat before hypnotizing me by playing his horn. He seemed different from the other kids there: kinder, more sensitive, almost other worldly. Later in life he would go on to attend Oakland's Public Conservatory of Music in California, and have an illustrious career as a trumpeter playing with the Boston Symphony Orchestra, Stanley Clarke, and Chick Corea among others.

When Mother moved us back to Detroit from Inkster it was to an upper flat on Kendall Street, in Madonna Parish, on the northwest side of town. But we didn't stay there long. Another expressway out of the city was being developed and so we had to go. Just like the Chrysler Freeway had uprooted Black Bottom, the Lodge was now en route to decimate our newly found terrain. But a few memories of that time have managed to survive.

There were lots of children in that area and we played outside endlessly jumping rope, playing hide and seek, tag, foot racing, and shooting marbles. Cat eyes were my favorite. When stuck inside we played pick-up sticks, jacks or with paper dolls.

Since Anita was the oldest, in Mother's absence, she was pretty much in charge. One evening, I remember, Mother was going to get her hair done and I didn't want her to go. I was probably about age five or six. Mother assured me that she'd just be down the street and left a phone number with my sister where she could be reached if necessary. I had protested and suggested a wide range of possibilities that might go wrong, but she reminded me that if I really got scared all I had to do was dial zero on the telephone for the police. Then she put us to bed and was off.

I awoke before she got back and was scared. It was dark inside and out. I cried and tried to wake up Nita but she was out for the count, so I fumbled my way to the phone, put my finger in the 0-hole and rotated the dial. The police were there within minutes, banging on the door and awaking my sleepy-headed sister who simply handed them the number Mother had left. Tears were still streaming down my face when she arrive a few moments later. While the two white officers seemed sympathetic to my plight, my mother, with only half her head in curls, was only somewhat bemused. I heard one of the men gently say to her, "I think the little one here just got scared." All I knew was I was happy to have her back home. And in the end she understood.

When the Lodge came, we moved two blocks over, still on Kendall but between Twelfth Street and Fourteenth, and into a lower flat this time numbered 1971. It is still directly behind the campus that then housed the church, school, convent, shrine and rectory named after the Madonna and Saint Paul (the fore-runner of both Focus Hope and the Catholic Church of Saint Moses the Black): the Parish seat and center of that community.

My sister and I attended school there kindergarten through eighth grade; and, although I didn't recognize it at the time, our lives were highly structured and quite provincial.

Mother had gotten a job as a Clerk Typist with the Army Tank Automotive Command, a branch of the Federal Government where she would remain some twenty-seven years. Before going to work each morning, she would prepare and leave breakfast for us. Most often, that consisted of oatmeal or cream-of-wheat left in the upper portion of a double boiler on top of the stove turned off. There would also be fresh squeezed orange juice for us to swallow our cod liver oil capsules with, and a loaf of bread (sometimes raisin bread) in case we wanted to make toast. In truth, many times the hot cereal got flushed and we considered the supplements optional.

Since we lived right behind the school, Nita and I seldom walked all the way down the block and around the corner to Oakman Boulevard. Instead, we simply cut through the property of the neighbor across the street and through the alley to the big green gate that provided access to the school grounds. Someone must have known that were doing this because the big, silver hook that kept that entryway shut was usually left unlatched.

Lots of people have horror tales about attending Catholic Schools and nuns who were too harsh or used corporal punishment, but I never witnessed nor experienced that. Madonna was a white school in an area that had become integrated but nonetheless stuck to its core educational curriculum and religious doctrines. Black parents who sent their children there did so to provide their kids with the best education they thought possible. Unlike residential schools that were specifically designed to strip non-whites of their culture, and where emersion was compulsory, attending a Catholic school was considered a privilege, although in both cases a Eurocentric assimilation was often the end result.

I remember the Sisters of Saint Joseph as being gentle, funny and kind. They wore long black dresses called habits; and stark white guimpe bibs, bandeaus and coifs topped off with long black veils; while even longer rosaries swung from around their waists. My favorite was Sister Marie Delores who introduced me to The Little World of Don Camillo; and, after I read that book, I knew it was okay for me to have direct conversations with God and to cut out the middle man.

Stories were always a big part of our upbringing. Mother read to us aloud from such classics as Tom Sawyer, Huckleberry Finn, Heidi and even Shakespeare, editing whatever she found offensive. She read Edgar Allen Poe's The Raven to us, and other narrative poem favorites like All's Well That Ends Well and The Cremation of Sam McGee. I can still remember big chunks of those today.

We didn't have a television for a long time when I was a kid. I don't think it was an affordability issue for mother so much as it just wasn't important to her. We listened to shows on the radio at night. There was Amos and Andy, Johnny Dollar and The Lone Ranger. Other times we practiced gymnastics or enacted passages from pieces we had read. My favorite-probably because it was one of Mother's favorites-was Mark Antony's famous monologue from Julius Caesar: *Friends, Romans, countrymen . . .* I would deliver it with great flare, jumping from floor to sofa to side chair, all the while brandishing an invisible sword that I used to hold back make-believe crowds. Once, in school, when I hadn't prepared an oral recitation homework assignment, I performed an impromptu version of that same speech to the bewilderment of my classmates but also the delight of the classroom nun.

Other forms of entertainment we enjoyed were evening walks along Oakman Boulevard to the Parkman Branch Library where we were allowed to check out as many books as we could carry without restrictions. Going and coming back, the game Nita and I played was picking out which houses we'd live in when we got older. The homes along that route were nearly comparable to those in the fabulous Boston-Edison District and each one was different from the next. Some were modern, some were like country cottages, others resembled castles or mini-mansions, and all of them were beautiful. We fanaticize about our future husbands and children and the lives that we would live. Sometimes we extended our walk to

Dexter Avenue just to keep the fantasies alive.

Other times, when Mother got home from work, we'd walk the opposite way on Oakman past the Yellow Pages Building and Sanders Bakery, and take Hamilton up to Pitkin Street where there was an even bigger playground than the one on Labelle behind our house. And sometimes we'd go over to the Canada Dry Bottling Plant on Third just to watch those glass cylinders cycle around on a conveyer belt. On ever rarer occasions, we'd make it all the way to the Sears store or Kresge's on Woodward Avenue where we'd sometimes get a treat before heading back home.

Not having a car in those days never really prevented us from getting anywhere we wanted to go. We walked or took buses that were strategically routed and usually on time. You could set your watch by them. Not many people in our neighborhood had cars back then, but those that did just might offer a ride. Of course you never accepted a ride unless you knew the driver. That was one of the rules of the realm, of this proverbial village of 1950s values in which many of my generation were raised.

Other prescripts dictated that, no matter what, you didn't lie because that always made matters worse. You shared your toys, boys didn't hit girls, big kids looked after little kids, and you never swore within earshot of an adult. No one ever littered; and, if an old person needed help with anything, you helped. And if they offered you money for doing it, you'd better not take it.

Our neighborhood was racially mixed back then which was incidental as far as I knew as a child. My sister's best friend, Diane Bowers, was white. There were still a few Jewish holdouts around. Tony, down on the corner, was Italian. One of my best friends, Vivian Zoma, was Chaldean. And next door, on one side folks were white while on the other side was a black family.

In that black house was my first ever crush, Zachary Edwards, and what impressed me most about him was how high he could climb the fruit tree in his back yard. He seemed fearless and I would try to copy him. But Mother kept cautioning me to stop traipsing after that bowlegged boy with the ashy knees. After his family moved away, I wouldn't meet up with him again until high school.

When I say our lives were structured, I mean like clockwork most of the time. Monday through Friday,

Nita and I got up and went to school and God forbid we should be late. Mother would know. After school, on certain days, one or the other of us would have a piano lesson with one of the nuns which meant both of us had to stay after. Then, as soon as we got home, we changed out of our uniforms into play clothes and hurried to do whatever chores Mother had left for us like pealing vegetables for dinner and setting the table, and then we got started on our homework.

Mother might rest a few moments, when she first got home from work, then she'd head into the kitchen and prepare the evening meal. Afterwards, while Mother checked our homework, Nita and I had alternating KP duty. One week, she washed the dishes and I dried; the next week it was the reverse. And whoever dried also had to sweep the floor. That was another rule. And only after all that was done could we enjoy some form of family entertainment.

Weekends were different. On Saturdays we had ballet lessons, followed by whatever shopping needed to be done, and cleaning the house in preparation for Sunday which was always considered a day of rest. Saturday nights were when we got scrubbed from head to toe. And on Sunday mornings it was off to Mass wearing our (sometimes matching) finest. Mother didn't go to Mass with us because, as a divorced Catholic, she believed herself to be excommunicated and therefore not allowed to receive the sacraments. After services, we'd come home and have a Sunday breakfast that might be pancakes, or sausages and scrambled eggs: something special. Then the day's pièce de résistance which might be a trip to one of the museums; or all the way downtown to one of the movie palaces like the Michigan, Fox or Grand Circus. All the great musicals, like Gypsy and West Side Story, were shown at grandiose establishments like these. Or it might be another walk to Highland Park but this time further up Woodward Avenue to either the Trans-Lux Krim Art House Theater where I was first introduced to Tosca, or the 6-Mile Uptown movies where second circuit movies were shown. And there were times, once we got our first television-a gift from a bailiff friend of Mother's-that we just stayed home to watch whatever Bill Kennedy was offering on the *boob-tube* while scarfing down potato chips followed by gulps of Squirt (Mother's favorite) or red pop.

During the summer months, when school was out, Nita and I went to summer camps. And not just for two week stints but for the whole summer. It was part of Mother's living mantra that her girls would not grow up in the streets.

I remember the first time. We took a long bus ride, along with a bunch of other kids I didn't know, to Guardian Angels Camp. I hated it straightaway. Immediately after being hurled into a huge dormitory, my escape plan began to hatch. I told Nita I wanted to go home but she was in a different dorm with girls closer to her age and remained unperturbed. So for two days I scoped out the landscape and clocked the hour lights were turned off; and, on the third night, I bundled up my possessions, hoisted them and myself up and out a side window, and hit the road.

The next day, when one of my mother's friends drove her all the way to camp to talk to me, the counselors explained that they found me walking along one of the trails in the dead of night but headed the wrong way. I thought I was going home.

Why? Mother wanted to know. I hated it, I explained. But she asked me to try it for at least a couple weeks, and arrangements were made for Nita and me to spend more time together. Eventually I adjusted, and the highlight of that summer turned out to be my discovery of black elderberries flowering wild just off the camp roads. They were wonderful and I ate them by the handfuls. It wouldn't be until my adult years that I'd learn they might have been poisonous.

We only attended Guardian Angels one year as I can recall. But another campground I remember was on Kelly's Island in Ohio. There, Nita and I were separated from the other campers and made to bunk together on the top floor of an old house. The reason, we were told, had to do with us both being asthmatic but not even Mother believed that. My worst memory of that place was when bats got into our dwelling space and Nita and I had to fight them off by snapping bath towels at them. We never went back there again.

The one camp that I remember fondly is Camp Cavell up in Lexington, Michigan, situated on Lake Huron. Nita and I went there several years in a row. It was where I was nicknamed Fergie and I swam, played softball, learned to fence with a foil, excelled at badminton, did archery, all sorts of arts and crafts, and got to ride horseback regularly-English style. And sometimes groups of us would go hiking, being careful not to touch the poison ivy of course, or we'd go into Croswell where we'd get to walk across its Swinging Bridge always on the lookout for notorious cherry pickers (migrant farm workers as we would learn later). Some of the friendships made there lasted several years and included winter reunions downtown at Big Boy's on Jefferson Avenue.

Back on Kendall Street, things were starting to change as more and more black families moved into the neighborhood. But the implications were not clear to me. From my perspective, it just meant there were more kids to play with, to help me key on my skates so I didn't have to bother Nita, or borrow a bike from since I didn't have one of my own. But then three incidents happened that made me stop and take notice. The first was when a girl at school stole my sweater and then lied about it. I'd never seen a person keep up a lie once they'd been caught in it out-right. The second time was when another person at school called me illegitimate. I didn't know what that meant but I knew it wasn't nice. And when I told Mother about it her reaction let me know it was not to be tolerated. She also assured me that I was just as legitimate as anyone else. The third event was even more telling.

Mother always bought us the best that she could, especially when it came to shoes. Most of the women in her family had bad feet and she was determined that such would not be our fate. We wore Buster Brown saddle oxfords to school, and fine patent leathers on Sundays. But as one particular Easter approached, after not finding what she could afford at the Hudson's store downtown, Mother walked us over to Crawley's budget basement. But the shoes there were rock hard, as she described them. So we got on another bus only to get off somewhere I didn't recognized, and were told by Mother to stand still on a corner and not to move while she huffed her way down the street. I watched her go up to the front door of a house and knock repeatedly until it was opened by my father who was wearing dark slacks and a white singlet. Although we couldn't hear a word she was saying, Mother seemed to be talking a million miles an hour as she put an opened hand out in front of her. My father's face looked angry but she kept talking. Then he raised his hand and hauled off and slapped her hard across her face. But still she kept talking, and kept her open hand out firm. Eventually, he went into his pocket and pulled out a wad of cash that he placed in her hand. Mother came back to where she had left us and we got on yet another bus that took us to Livernois-The Avenue of Fashion-where she bought us fine new, black, patent leather Easter shoes. I remember feeling proud that she'd held her ground.

During this period from the mid-50s to the early 60s, Nita and I were steeped in Catholicism. We made our First Communions wearing the same handed-down dress and veil, carefully selected our Confirmation names, and I even got to carry a flowered head-wreath on a pillow for May Crowning one spring. But something new was permeating the air: a deeper cadence that was unlike the sanctity of the Latin hymns we'd grown up with. A richer deliverance of truths that was proving to be ecumenical. As usual, I asked questions but for the most part I was ignored.

Some of the other kids in the neighborhood had grown up in the south or had family there and often returned there during summer months, but not Nita and me. As far as I knew, slavery, racism and discrimination were things that had happened in the long ago past but now everyone was free and equal. It never occurred to me than anyone would think any of us were less than or inferior to them based on our skin color. Still, that pulsating drumbeat that was Reverend Martin Luther King, Jr's voice drew me in. And not just me, it seemed everyone was suddenly hanging on the words of this Baptist minister. The more questions I asked, the more I got shushed and so I looked for information in newspapers and magazines but the more I read the more confusing it all seemed: my upbringing vs. these new realities of the world. Like most folk around me, I did the best I could with what I understood.

It was the men in Mother's life, all of whom were gentlemen (excluding my own father) who brought new sensibilities into my life: They took Nita and me on many of their dates with her, at her insistence no doubt. She was a love-me-love-my-children kind of mom. When we didn't accompany them, they brought back doggy bags of delights we had never been exposed to before. And they had cars and would pick us up for Sunday outings to Palmer Park or Belle Isle where, to get there, we would go through an underground tunnel from East Grand Boulevard to get to the island. And sometimes, they'd take us with them on midnight rides to pick up the last batch of visitors at the Bob-Lo Amusement Park. On that last run, you didn't get off the boat, you just road over and came right back (at a reduce fare no doubt); but, on the ride back, the band would still play and we'd watch Mother dance and she was good-really good-attracting onlookers. It was amazing to me. She'd have on a white blouse with puffy, shear sleeves and a cat pin on its round collar; and a wide, black, taffeta, tea length skirt with a colorful petticoat underneath, the hem of which you could see as she twirled.

Although there was a clear line of demarcation between the worlds of adults and children then, as a girl, I did pick up on some of what was going on in the broader regions. Mother's men friends talked about topics she never broached with us like race, war and sports, especially one brash young fighter named Cassius Clay who kept saying that he was so pretty. The first time I saw a picture of him I thought, *He's my complexion; so if he's pretty, I must be pretty too.* Prior to that, all the prettiness accolades had been heaped upon my sister and I had just accepted that as her status while mine remained nonplussed. But with Clay as a role model, I found I could hold my own against adolescent bullies who sneeringly called me *yellow* or accused me of thinking I was better than them simply because I might be a shade lighter than they. Then, when Clay changed his name to Mahammad Ali, and later refused to go to Vietnam, he-along with Dr. King's stance on the war-helped shape my own political views.

By the time I followed Nita to Visitation High School, which was considered one of the best Catholic high schools in the city, she was a Junior and had already established herself as a good student who was also talented. She sang, danced, and played the guitar in addition to getting good grades. The nuns loved her and expected me to be just like her. But good grades didn't come easily to me. I had to study to get them.

One subject that was particularly hard for me was Latin, a required class for all Visi students. And one morning, my Freshman year, as I slowly walked up the isle to take my seat in Sister Innocentia's room, keenly aware that I was ill prepared for the test we were about to have, I silently prayed with all my heart that some miracle would occur so I wouldn't have to take it.

Just then an announcement came over the loud speaker telling us that President John F. Kennedy had been shot. Everyone was shocked. As for me, I looked up toward the heavens and whispered in my mind: *God, I didn't mean that.* All of us then sat down and prayed until the second announcement came that in fact the President had died, and then the entire school was dismissed. No one who was alive on that infamous November 22nd in 1963 ever forgets where they were and what they were doing when they heard that fateful news. It was truly the beginning of an end to a nation-wide naiveté that had enveloped so many of us with regard to underpinning of politics in these United States.

Nita graduated in 1965 and went on to attend Mercy College. She also took voice training in opera, successfully launched a modeling career, and competed in local beauty pageants like Miss Hot Pants and Miss Detroit. And it was great fun to watch her. In those days, the tendency for parents was to get the first born firmly on path in a direction before turning their attention to the next in line, and that worked just fine for me. It left me free to develop my own interests and establish my own persona which I did: a bit of a prankster, an avid reader, adventurous and wanting to be a writer. I also loved movies and got my first job, at age sixteen, as a Candy Girl at the Studio New Center, a newly established art-house cinema on Third Avenue across from the Fisher Building. It was the latest in a chain of Studio Theatres that included the original Studio One on Livernois near Davison, the Studio North or Woodward near 9 Mile Road, and the Studio 8 on Greenfield in Southfield.

With a couple exceptions, the staff at the Studio New Center were students at Wayne State University. There was Gordon Mayer, Steve Bennett, Diane Evangelistica, Larry Stewart, Chuck Black, and Freddie Frank.

Gordon was the oldest and seemed to me the epitome of sophistication. My best friend at the time, Christine Szypulski, had a tremendous crush on him. As it turned out, he had once been the boyfriend of one of my camp counselors (Penny) at Camp Cavell.

Steve Bennett was my crush. He was 6'2, 220lbs, blond with blue eyes. I could barely breathe when he was around me. In truth, I'd let my cigarettes burn out rather take a puff whenever he was near for fear that I might choke in his presence.

I’m not sure what happened to Diane Evangelistica or even that I’m spelling her name correctly here, but I think I may have been her replacement in the box office when she left. I remember her as being beautiful with long, black, flowing hair, and very kind and gracious. She was the first female I ever met who let me know that one of the guys had an interest in me. When I think of her today, I imagine she’s a doctor.

Larry Stewart was handsome, also with dark hair and lots of personality. And I remember a stolen kiss in the Manager’s Office with him that was probably my first.

And then there was Fred Frank, the nicest guy in the world. I think he may have had a crush on me while I thought of him as a friend. He was easy to be around and we talked and laughed a lot together. We exchanged gifts (Christmas/Hanukkah). I remember him giving me a bottle of J&B scotch while I gave him a James Brown album. He also took me to Synagogue once, and cooked dinner for me another time at his house when his parents were away.

But Chuck Black probably had the most influence on me and I’m sure he never even knew it. He was the ticket taker in the theatre lobby and one of the exceptions to Wayne State. He was attending community college. He shared the whys and wherefores of his plan of transferring to a four year school once he finished his current studies, which were easier and considerable cheaper.

While, in my heart, I wanted to go to WSU like the cool kids, ultimately I would follow a path much more similar to Chuck's. But in the meantime, I soaked up everything I could from the chatter at work about politics, the Vietnam War, and the art-worthiness of certain films. By the time I graduated from high school, in 1967, I was more convinced than ever that I was going to be a writer.

My class was the last class to graduate from Visitation High School. Once we were gone, the school's name changed to honor Saint Martin DePorres. But that was hardly the most notable thing that happened that year in Detroit.

During the winter months, when my sister was working at the Roostertail Night Club downtown, she met and became involved with one of the radio DJs on the Canadian station CKLW. I met him once when he had driven her home from work but I didn't care for his cocky personality. Later in the year, around the time of the Vernal Equinox, when

Alfred, Lord Tennyson would have us believe young men's fancies turn to thoughts of love, another young man took matters into his own hands. My sister had gotten the bus home from work that evening/early a.m., and he followed her when she got off at her stop, dragged her into an alley and raped her.

Imagine her terror.

And when it was learned that she was pregnant, the question became: who was the biological father? It was a black and white issue that would take nine months to be resolved.

Mother was beside herself. All her dreams for her first born were headed down the drain. She didn't want Nita to keep the baby but my sister refused to let go.

In the meantime, I was having my own battle with Mother by refusing to follow in my sister's footsteps to Mercy College. I had long wanted to get away from the Catholic school system and go to what I considered "real school." I told her I wanted to go to Wayne State. Her contention was that I would never be accepted there and for some reason I took that to heart. She also said that Mercy was the only school for which she was willing to pay.

I thought of Chuck Black, devised my own plan, applied to Highland Park Community College, and started saving every penny I could. I also went down to the Detroit Urban League, begged for their support, and they graciously sent me a check for one hundred dollars. By the time of my high school graduation, and after I got over my father not showing up for it despite his promise that he'd be there, I had a clearer vision of my future and felt like I was on my way. Then the next month came the riots.

Most everyone is our surrounding area called the '67 uprising a riot back then. That was how it was described in the newspapers. It broke out just a few blocks south of where Nita and I had gone school, and then moved upward toward our neighborhood. We were in shock, traumatized. We didn't know what to make of the violence, looting, racial vitriol, or the National Guard troops patrolling the streets, or what happened at the Algiers Motel. We also knew very little of the racial history of our own city and it would take years of self-education to help remedy that.

By the time things settled down, I was studying hard at HPCC, still working in the box office at the movie house, and cashiering part time at the Sears store near the school.

Then, on December 19, 1967, my nephew Shannon was born and there was no longer any question about his parentage. As a first name he was given his father's surname. The first time I saw him he was wrapped up in a blanket and I remember saying he was as cute as a bug, so that became my nickname for him-*Bug*.

My sister was in a whirl. Lawyers had stepped in, papers were being drawn up, some money was exchanging hands. I just watched from the sidelines, until a light started shinning on me.

I caught that gleam in my mother's eye because I had seen it before. Earlier in that year, unbeknownst to me, she had submitted my picture for a fashion contest sponsored by Ingénue Magazine and I had been selected a finalist. I was furious when I found out. My photo, along with the other chosen ones, was on display in one of the windows in Crowley Milner's store downtown. And the final competition-a fashion show-was scheduled for the same weekend as my school's Senior Class Trip to Washington, D.C. no less. It was as if Mother had suddenly realized she had a second daughter to foist her own dreams onto now that Nita was out of commission.

Mother carried on about that contest, and since I had no money of my own for the trip, I felt I had no choice but to comply. I didn't win, of course, and I remember sticking my tongue out at the audience on my final trip down the runway.

Modeling was not my thing. That dream belonged to Nita. I wanted to be a writer, so after that I kept my head down and kept reading and writing until I mustered up enough courage to send out some of my work. But I never got any takers.

Write what you know, is what my English teachers said, but I always felt I didn't know much. I hadn't lived or done anything worth writing about. I was just an amiable kid, with an active imagination, who liked to read, wanted to see the world, and had grandiose dreams of being a writer one day.

The Big Apple and Beyond

1968 was a watershed year for me. Reverend King was killed in April of that year and I marched, along with other HPCC students, from our school down to Wayne State in order to have our outrage noted. Two months later Bobby Kennedy was killed. There was a lot of tension on Kendall Street between Mother and Nita. My heartthrob from the movies had gone off into the military and I was scared he might die in Nam until I learned he was in fact in Officers Candidate School. My own studies weren't going as well as I had hoped and my German language teacher was trying to expel me from his class while another teacher was trying to sleep with me. I hated going home, so Chris and I spent a lot of time at a coffee shop near school where we came up with a plan for a revitalizing summer adventure. I'd already been to Plum Street with a fellow classmate named Cornell Colbert; to me, it was like a mini version of what was happening in San Francisco. So let's go there, I said, to the mecca of it all. This was, after all, supposed to be the *Age of Aquarius*, of peace and love.

That dream kept me going and, at home by myself, I would play pack a suitcase with what I would take when the time came. Then one day Mother came home early from work and interrupted me, and I quickly hid the suitcase under my bed. She was in a huff about something that had to do with Nita and I was just tired of hearing about it. So I said I had to be at work early and left the house. The next day, after withdrawing the little money Chris and I had jointly saved up at a bank, I wrote apologies to her, resignations to both my bosses, a good-bye note to Mother; and I grabbed that suitcase, went down to the Greyhound Bus Terminal, and bought a one way ticket to the Golden Gate Bay area.

There was an hour wait before departure so I sat in the café there, drank coffee, and listened to a juke box recording of Sunday in New York. I thought it was Tony Bennett singing at the time but with hindsight it was probably Mel Torme: *troubles bursting like bubbles in a big city taking a nap.* I also started thinking that if I went to California, the hot spot for that year, I'd probably run into the same people I already knew from Detroit. So I changed my ticket for a cheaper one that was leaving in ten minutes for New York, and by the wee hours of the next morning I was awakening to the sight of Big Apple bright lights.

It was a rough trip getting there, but even rougher when I first got off the bus and was approached by a dapper-looking probable pimp who wanted to know whether I had some place to stay. I sensed his intentions weren't honorable, so I went up to the uniformed cop on the corner and told him that the man was bothering me. What did he say to you, the cop wanted to know. And when I told him, his response was, "Well, do you have some place to stay?"

Hello New York!

The streets were dirty and grimy. I went inside the Port Authority building where I met a hippy couple who warned me not to loiter or I'd be arrested. They suggested I put my bag in a locker and then invited me to hang out with them until it got light outside. Their bus for the west coast wasn't leaving until 7:00 a.m. and, in the meantime, they were going to pull one more all-nighter riding the subway trains. It was my first introduction to the underground world of the city. By the time they left me, I had put together my own sort of plan and was lugging my suitcase up to the west side YWCA when a man offered to help me. When I told him I was looking for a job, he told me about an opening for a

Hat Check Girl at the Tin Lizzy which sounded like a pretty fancy restaurant. I thought of Nita at the Roostertail and, the next afternoon, went there and got hired. But the man who had made the referral seemed to think that my gratitude to him should include moving in with him and becoming *his girl*. But that wasn't going to work for me so I got out of there after my third night on the job.

With little more than $100- to my name, and one week's rent at the Y was going to take half of that, I knew I had to find another job aswellas cheaper living accommodations. And so I did.

It was easy to do back then. I picked up a daily newspaper, went through the want ads, circled a few, and started making phone calls for interviews. The first firm that hired me was down near the Village. It was the offices for a company that made Rainmates, those little, accordion-like, plastic head coverings that women carried in their purses to protect their coifs during unexpected showers. But I left there in a huff after a week or two when the big boss screamed at me for some slight infraction. I simply wasn't used to being treated that way.

Growing up without a father in the home, and under the protective watch of my mother, no man had ever raised a gruff voice to me. I'd never experienced first-hand the male ego in full rage and I certainly wasn't prepared to accept it. Besides, jobs were easy to come by back then so I simply got another. I worked at Tiffany's for a while, and at Georg Jensen's Christmas Shop, at an upscale movie house where they had Hollywood premiers, and down in the Village at the Andy Warhol Theatre for a minute.

Talk about extremes.

By the time I met the man that I would marry, I was living at the Lancaster Hotel on 38th Street and Madison, and working days as a cashier in the coffee shop there, and as a receptionist part time at its sister hotel, the Seaton, on 40th and Park. All of this had been arranged for me by the Lancaster's manager as a kind gesture to ensure I paid my rent, and so he wouldn't have to plug my lock. As an employee I got a discounted rate and free food. In exchange, I would also babysit for him and his wife so that they could enjoy an occasional evening out, and I played hostess for them for some of their more formal occasions. They were Syrian, and the wife would dress me up in one of her exquisite outfits that made me look so stunning that I hardly recognized myself.

My best friend in those days was a young woman named Ernestine Johnson that I met when we both had worked together at Georg Jensen's. Ernie lived in the Bronx with her fiancée, Craig, who worked an afternoon shift there. So when she got off from work, she'd often hang out with me and catch a late train home so that she and he would get there around the same time.

Ernie was pregnant, which led the couple to speed up their wedding date, and Craig to work as many hours as he could in preparation for starting this new family. Then suddenly, without warning, Ernie lost the baby and they were both devastated. She kept wondering whether she had done something wrong. She'd had stomach cramps, she said, and went to the bathroom and while sitting there on the toilet, there'd been a big whoosh followed by a lot of blood and the fetus falling away from her. The pain, both psychological and physical, sent her into an understandable funk. Afraid to be alone, she continued going to work and then coming to me until time to take a late train home.

To kill time and to cheer her up, we'd do some of the old things we used to do like window shopping or taking silly pictures in photo booths. Then one night, we stopped into an eatery on 42nd Street call Nell Gwynn's where "*Kissin' don't last but cookery do.*" was the caption, and where Brian happened to be working.

Undoubtedly, he was a good judge of people and seem to sense Ernie's sadness immediately. He charmed her, made her smile, made her laugh. I wasn't overly impressed with him myself but I was delighted that he made my friend happy. He told us that he was from Liverpool in England (not that we didn't recognize his Beatle-ish accent), had been in the Merchant Marines (whatever that was), was currently a songwriter, and kept us captivated with tales from afar. We stayed there so long that, in the end, Ernie and I had to bolt for her to make her train.

The next week Ernie wanted to go back there and this time he turned the charm on me as well, sprinting with us to the subway, and then insisting on walking me home.

It was probably another a week and a half, and a few phone calls later, before I agreed to go out with him. I had told him about a time when a friend of my sister's had come to town and taken me to The Copacabana and, to get in, we had gone through a secret entrance via a hotel next door to the club. I'd gone back a second time, the same way, with a Norwegian friend named Gunnar for an opening night Tony Bennett show. Brian wanted to try it and so voila, I was back at The Copa to see Tony Bennett once again.

After that we seemed to go everywhere: dinners at nice restaurants, museums, and Broadway plays followed by drinks at the 8th Avenue Haymarket. I would only learn later-much later-that the restaurant dinners were at places where his friends worked, and where they charged our bill to other customer's credit cards.

But in the meantime, during those blissful days of innocence when I thought everything was on the up-and-up, I enjoyed the whirlwind effects of a courtship I'd never known before. I had a boyfriend for the first time ever. We talked, had both been raised Catholic, had comparable writing dreams, loved living in the city, went places and did things together. So when Brian said we should get married, and I phoned home to tell Mother, and she was so delighted that at least one of her daughters was getting married and wasn't even pregnant, I felt as if the die had been cast.

Mother stayed in high gear and, in addition to buying my wedding dress, she also bought an engagement ring that she sent to Brian to give to me, and made arrangements for my sister, nephew, and for her to come to New York for the big day.

Brian's mates took care of the local details and he and I were married before a Justice of the Peace upstate in Orangeburg, NY on April 19, 1969. I was still but only 19 years of age.

Mother was always charmed by Brian

We never went on a honeymoon, we moved into The Seaton instead and went back to work immediately. Brian was bartending, and I had a job as a receptionist for the architects Hausman and Rosenberg, two of the nicest gentlemen I'd ever know, and who saw right through the façade of the life I thought I was living and tried to warned me the first time I showed up for work bruised.

Growing up, there had never been any doubt in my mind that my mother loved both my sister and me. She spanked us to be sure, but it was as a means of discipline never of malice. She laid down rules that, as long as we lived under her roof we was obliged to follow; if we didn't, there were consequences. It was a simple matter of cause and effect that she talked to us about at length.

So when Brian apologized, explained his behavior as a result of being under the influence of alcohol, and promised never to raise a hand to me again, being the good Catholic girl that I was, I accepted that and was forgiving. Not that my hackles weren't raised a few times after that in the midst of verbal arguments with him.

I began to see clearly that he had a mean streak. But I'd been raised to speak my mind, and I had held my own against Nita, and nuns, and even Mother although always with the utmost respect. So I didn't hold back when problems arose with him but I did try to compromise, consider his advice, or come up with creative solutions that would satisfy us both. We tried to work things out.

After a hit and miss beginning, the romance went back to much the way it had been when we were dating. We continued to doubled-up with Brian's friends Jackie Grant and his girlfriend Joan. We still hung out with the gang at The Haymarket where they got real excited when one of the lads, Michael Cahill, landed a role in the play Borstal Boy and got an excellent review as a result. We saw lots of other Broadway shows as well: Hadrian VII, Company, Nicol Williamson doing Hamlet, Pearl Bailey in Hello Dolly.

By August I discovered I was pregnant with our first child and we were both excited. It was all an adventure to me, but to Brian it seemed like a second chance for him to make good. He'd been married before, in 1956, at St. Augustine's Church in Liverpool to a woman that he had gotten pregnant named Ann Devaney. But that union had been officially dissolved back in January of 1964. This time, and under different circumstances, he was trying to do everything right.

He knew The Seaton was too small, so he found us a balcony apartment at 355 Mayflower Avenue in New Rochelle. He also found a better job tending bar at The Plaza Hotel.

Michelle Chante was born May 7, 1970, at 6:23 p.m. She weighed 7 lbs. 9 oz. and was 22″ long. Brian wasn't at the hospital at the time of her birth but came to see her as soon as he got then news then went off to The Haymarket to celebrate.

One week later, she and I were testing each other out at home to see who was actually going to run the show. She was a beautiful baby and I loved her dearly but sometimes she cried and I couldn't figure out why. I'd feed her, burp her, change her, cradle and rock her but still she cried. In my frustration, I'd start crying too. How was I going to be a good mother if I couldn't figure out why my baby was crying? Then all of a sudden she'd stop, look up at me and smile. Then she'd fall asleep. It was baffling.

The problems would escalated when Brian got home from work. He was on afternoons at the Plaza and always had a time crunch when he got off to catch a slow-rolling Westchester train to get home. If he missed that train, which sometimes he did, the next one wouldn't be until the early morning hours.

Sometimes when he got home, Michelle would start crying. He'd yell at me to keep her quiet and if I couldn't he go into a rage. He needed his sleep. The yells would turn into screams that made the baby cry all the more. He'd accuse me of being an incompetent mother and, eventually, of keeping the baby awake all day so that she'd purposely cry at night just to disturb him. I was already feeling demoralized, and after two weeks of his nonsense, with my hackles at full mast, I'd had it. I packed some of Michelle and my belongings, slipped off my wedding ring, and got on a plane that was headed to San Francisco.

The difference from east coast to west was palpable to me from the beginning. Most of the people I talked to on that flight were going home. They all cooed over my baby. They were friendly, they chit-chatted with me and offered advice and recommendations when they learned this was my first trip to the Bay area. The guy sitting next to me offered me a ride from the airport to the hotel most passengers said would be a good starting point for me. And I took him up on it. A week later he came by just to check on me.

When Brian and I first married we'd opened a joint banking account. When I left New York, I took half of what was in it with me. And with that, things progressed smoothly for me. I found a nice studio apartment with a huge closet that I converted into a room for Michelle, and was busily checking want ads for a job when I saw one in the PERSONAL's column with my name on it. It spake of Brian's undying love for me, told how everyone was worried about me, and urged me to call either him or my mother. I thought about what I had done and felt guilty. I called home.

Mother talked about my obligation to my child not deny her a father in her life. She was able to convince me to, at least, call Brian and I did. He cried, and worked hard to persuade me to come back and so, for Michelle's sake, I did.

But I could see from the moment I returned a clear difference between what he said and his body language. True, he had been hurt and was happy to have us back, but he was also angry. Very angry.

Brian considered that the money I had taken out of the bank I had stolen from him. Although I gave back what was left of that lot, he always held that against me. As for me, I vowed never to be completely dependent on anyone for cash ever again. Even Mother had instilled that in me. She had often given me fine pieces of jewelry as birthday presents and the like, and they were usually accompanied with a premonitions reminder that they could always be pawned if necessary.

The Westchester railroad was notoriously slow and/or late and the butt of many late night television jokes. Brian claimed it was the bane of his after work existence. His solution, as the Mayflower lease neared expiration, was to find us a flat closer to Manhattan. It was in Astoria, Queens, Long Island City, and a mere twenty minute ride away on an El. I never saw the place beforehand, but Brian assured me it would be perfect with a large living room, full kitchen and two bedrooms.

The landlords, Max and Leah Wolfe, lived downstairs and owned a bakery across the street. They were Holocaust survivors. Since they hadn't met me beforehand, they were surprised to see that I was black; or rather, they weren't sure and chose not to believe it. They told all the neighbors that I was ". . . from the islands." I was already making twice weekly visits to their shop as their bread was absolutely incredible; and when I found out their lie, I took time to fluff and pick my hair out, put on a dashiki top and linger in their store until they got the message and eventually apologized. Of course they fell in love with Michelle, even volunteered to babysit, and Max spent endless hours telling me horror tales about his imprisonment, and explaining different Jewish traditions.

When we moved in there, we had done so with the idea of saving up for a year and then moving to England. The exchange rate on the pound was very good at that time, and Brian was convinced that if we saved hard, we'd be able to put a down payment on a house there, something we'd never be able to do in New York City.

So we saved. I was already frugal, and an added advantage was that we were living in a predominately Italian neighborhood where food prices seemed to be regulated for that community. Plus, right down the street from us was a bar where it was claimed that Tony Bennett had gotten his start. We spent a few social evening there.

Five predictive episodes now stick out in my mind from that period before we moved to Liverpool.

The first was when Michelle was christened. One of Brian's coworkers had a baby about the same age so we agreed to have a joint celebration. There was lots of food and drink, and as the boys' tongues loosened, I caught snippets of tales from their jobs about various customer requests; in particular, for prostitutes. But as my ears perked up, the conversation shifted. I asked Brian about it later and he claimed innocence but I never believed him.

Another time, when Brian was at work and I was home doing a closet purge, I came across a huge wad of cash that he had hidden away. I don't remember now how much it was; I'm not even sure I counted it all, but it was certainly several hundred dollars and maybe more.

The third shocker came to me over the telephone. It rang one day, I answered it, and a male voice identified himself to me as my brother. I don't have a brother, I told him. Yes you do, he insisted and he claimed to be Harold Ferguson, Jr.

Growing up I knew I had at least two half-sisters, Rhonda and another younger Karen that was frequently referred to as "*Little Karen*" to distinguish her from me, but I'd never heard tale of a brother.

I tracked down my father's phone number and called him. I told him about the phone call I'd received and asked him if he knew who the guy was. His response was simple. Sure, he said, he's your brother.

Say what?!!

As we got closer to our departure date, there were still a few odds and ends lingering. One was a desk that we had bought brand new and shared. He used it to work on songs, I used it to write poems and other short pieces. It was symbolic of our dreams and what we had in common. When we got a final mere offer of $25- I was offended. But Brian grabbed at it and patted me on my head.

Soon we were off. And, as we were deplaning at Heathrow Airport, Brian pulled me aside and told me to use a makeshift address that he handed me if the Custom Officers asked where we were staying. Why? I wanted to know. I thought we were staying with his sister. Brian got nervous with my questioning and finally admitted that he had written a bogus check for our airfare.

The word shocked doesn't adequately describe what I felt when he told me that. A million thoughts suddenly started running through mind but in no appreciable order: why he had done that; the wad of cash from the closet; whose address was on the piece of paper; would we be arrested? Luckily the official spoke only to Brian and, after checking and stamping our passports, welcomed him back home.

It was a three hour train ride from London to Liverpool during which Brian kept apologizing. He'd never do it again, he promised, but I was too tired to try to believe him. I coddled, fed and played with Michelle until the two of us fell asleep.

Once at Vera's, Brian's sister, I spent a lot of time just smiling and nodding. Their way of speaking wasn't anything like what I'd heard in London. I could barely understand what they were saying. Their cadences were sing-songy and they spoke so fast.

We stayed there two or three weeks, then were off on holiday to Mallorca, Spain, where I was spellbound by the beauty of the Mediterranean and all my cares and worries seemed to slip away.

Back in Britain two weeks after that, we lived in the horror house that was Brian's mom's. This woman seemed to think that I was there to serve and wait on her. Had I understood the role that Liverpool played in the slave trade industry ages ago, I might have had a better understanding of her attitude, but this was all new to me. She expected me to build coal fires, squeeze water out of her laundry with a hand ringer, shop for her, polish her wood-work and mirrors with a chamois leather, and get down on my hands and knees to pick specks of dust from the corners of her stairs.

I blew up, first at her then at Brian. Her only reaction was to say she was glad Brian had married someone who would stand up to him.

Shortly after that, we moved into the house Brian had gotten for us. It was a two-up-and-two-down at One Adamson Street, in a in a cul-de-sac off Edge Lane in Fairfield, Liverpool 7. And a new adventure began.

Although Brian was driving a taxi at night, he had lots of creative ideas that I encouraged. He set up an office in town and tried selling ads that would go on the underside of cab seats and show when they were flipped up. He made terry cloth nappies, pink on one side and blue on the other, curved like U.S. Pampers. He sold Amway, and wrote a little novelty book called, "Lern Yerself Scouse. Wersia Sensa Yuma?" But as with any entrepreneur, things didn't go as easily as he had expected, and he took it out on me.

Money was tight and my solution was to get a part time job. But Brian seemed embarrassed to have his wife working. His solution was to strum his guitar and drink. He'd had a couple minor musical successes with two songs he'd written in New York: The Magic of Christmas and Misguided Faith, and he felt sure he was poised for another. But the more he drank, the deeper he slunk into what I perceived as depression. I'd try to talk him out of it but that only lead to arguments, and sometimes physical fights in which I tried to give back whatever I got from him. Undoubtedly I'd have been better off if I'd just kept my mouth shut, but I hadn't learned that yet.

By 1973 I was pregnant with our second child. Daniel was born on November 7th at 6:23 a.m. and was the exact same weight and length as his sister had been. Everyone was delighted. But unlike his sister, who I have long described as being like a text book baby-she did everything pretty much on schedule-this boy child ran his own course. He was so high energy that the doctors called him hyper and suggested medication but I wouldn’t allow that. I figured I could keep up with him.

Things were better on the home front, but a big part of that had to with me and the kids being away from the home during the day when Brian slept, and him driving his taxi afternoons and evenings when we were there. He also pretty much stopped drinking, but seemed to replace the booze with a kind of hypochondria. Still, we managed to vacation in the Isle of Mann and even bring in the New Year a couple more times before everything went completely south.

It had been building up for a long time. I’d learned so much more about him. His undying admiration for the disgraced former footballer Tony Kay who he claimed as a close friend of his; an equal amount of respect for all the gang of the Great Train Robbery of 1963 in London; that he himself had spent time in prison for safecracking after having been caught hiding in a cabbage patch. He had also been banned from the Merchant Navy after a man with whom he’d had a fight died. And then one night he tried to convince me that the world would be a better off if I was dead: he wanted me to kill myself, like his own father had done. He had already poisoned a neighbor's dog for disturbing his sleep, so I wasn't sure what he might try to do to me next. I just knew I had to get the kids and me away.

The last big fight we had I'd taken them and went to Vera's. I was trying to get back home. But he found us there and snatched Michelle away and, unwilling to leave one of my children behind, I went back to Adamson Street. But by now I had learned my lesson.

I kept my mouth shut and went about old daily routines as if all our problems were obliterated; then, one quiet afternoon, I gathered up the kids and a few belonging for each of us, whatever cash I had in the bank, my jewelry and hightailed it out of there.

Family Matters

Surprisingly, Mother came through for us. I called her from Heathrow and asked her to arrange for our flight home on her end and she did. Even more surprising was seeing Uncle Bobby by her side when we got there.

Detroit wasn't anything like I remembered it from growing up there. Continuing *white flight* and middle class black abandonment had left it in a deplorable state. Even Liverpool, which was also an industrial city that still had bombed-out shelters from WWII, looked better than Motown did then. I began to wonder whether I had made a mistake coming back. But then the instantaneous relief I felt being on my own turf was all too reassuring. And even the kids seemed more at ease and relaxed.

Of course, everyone was mesmerized by them. It would be years later before anyone would admit to me they couldn't understand a word they were saying. Some people also thought that I had picked up a bit of an accent.

Silly.

I told Mother not to tell Brian that she had heard from us if he called, but she did just the opposite and within three weeks he was there pleading his case and for more forgiveness.

And it never ceased to amaze me how Brian was able to do the things he did. He got a job right away, rented a place to stay on Gulley Road in Dearborn, bought himself a car, and continued charming Mother by bringing in food for us all and acting like more of a father to the kids than he had ever done in England.

Of course some of it was my fault. I had never told Mother all the gory details of my married life with Brian, and so she remained optimistic that our union would survive and was even trying to facilitate that. And since I had always taught the kids to be respectful their father, just as I tended to do in front of them, and just as Mother had insisted of Nita and me with our dad when we were youngsters, it's no wonder that he easily succeeded.

Brian had money to spend because he'd sold the house on Adamson Street before he came. And he was allowed to stay here because he told Immigration that he was married to American which was true at the time. But I doubt that really would have made much of a difference because, as I found out later, when I first met Brian he had simply overstayed his original three week visa. One way or another, he was determined to get what he wanted. And what he wanted now was to get us all back in his clutches.

He was solicitous. All of a sudden he had so much concern for the kid's and my wellbeing. He begged to stay a part of our lives. Although I refused to go back with him, I did encourage him to engage with the children and included him in family activities.

From the onset, however, neither my father nor Uncle Bobby trusted him, and it was like they were always circling him, sizing him up, feeling him out with a certain sense of knowing. And the air would thicken with tension whenever he was under the same roof with either.

It was interesting seeing so much of my father then-this man who had been practically absent from my life when I was growing up-but he wasn't really there for my benefit. He had been on the Kendall horizon for the past ten years for my nephew's sake.

Nita had been dealt a crushing blow when Tom Shannon wrote her off. After her son was born, with Mother's help, she tried to revive her modeling career aswellas the glamorous night life that often went along with it.

That left a lot of the raising of her boy child to Mother who was still working her clerical government job. Dad stepped in to help. He was a man's man who claimed to know just what the boy needed.

So, too, Uncle Bobby. Sort of.

As a youngster, I kind of glamourized my mother's brother whenever he came around which wasn't often either. But that was by Mother's choice. She didn't want him around. To me he was like a black Edward G. Robinson: rough, tough and TV gangster-ish. In truth, he was a gangster who spent a lot of my youth incarcerated.

Dad helped me buy what was then a HUD house at 14209 Prevost Street in St. Mary's of Redford Parish. Mother lent me the down payment. It was a three bedroom colonial with a fireplace; another remnant of urban withdrawal; but, compared to where Brian was living, a mansion.

Michelle was enrolled in school and Dan went to an on campus Drop-In Day Care while I took classes at Wayne State University. Two of my classes were on Saturday so it had been established that Brian would pick up the kids Friday when he got off work and keep them until Sunday afternoon when he would bring them home.

But one weekend, as I walked into the vestibule of the house Saturday after classes, I knew immediately that something was wrong. There was a ray of sunlight streaming from the coat closet door that had been left ajar. And I knew I had closed that door that morning. I opened it the rest of the way. All the kid's coats were gone. I ran upstairs to their bedrooms. Their clothes and toys were gone. It hit me in a flash that Brian had been back in the house, taken the kid's things, and run off with them.

Michelle had a key to the house around her neck in case of an emergency and Brian knew that. He also knew my schedule: the buses I took, my class locations, the time I usually got home; again, in case of an emergency. Unwittingly, I had given him everything he needed to plan a perfect kidnapping.

The police said I had to wait twenty-four hours before I could file a missing person's report. They also reminded me repeatedly that, as their father, Brian had just as much right to them as I did. It didn't seem to matter to them that, while our divorce was pending, I had been granted temporary custody.

Dad knew a lawyer he thought would help me. When my father used to run "*joints*" he catered to the upper echelon of the local black community and still maintained relationships with some of them. He referred me to attorney Ed Bell, a former judge.

Nita knew a current judge that she'd met at one of the clubs where she had worked. He played a mean jazz piano there some nights, probably to relax from his day job. She called him.

Mother kept saying that Brian would bring the kids back. Like to local police, she didn't believe that he intended to keep them; that he had just taken them to hurt me and would be back in a day or two.

I stayed on the phone calling Brian's home, his place of employment, the church where he'd been baptized on the east side of the city, his sister Vera back in England. I got nothing. It seemed nobody knew anything and all I could do was wait.

Three days straight I waited, sitting in front of the living room window so I could see them as soon as they came back. I didn't eat or sleep; I drank coffee and smoked cigarettes. And I made periodic runs back to the police station to check whether they'd had any success but the answer was always no.

That third night, at the insistence of my father, I was ushered upstairs to shower and then to bed. And during that night I had a dream. In it, I could see Michelle's face clearly. Her hair was in ringlets framing her face and I awoke with a knowing that she would look just like that when I found her-and that would be soon-and that, get the kids back, I would. There was not any doubt in my mind about it.

Then the fourth day, I spotted something that had been before my eyes the whole time but I hadn't seen it. A white, business size envelope tucked between photos displayed on the living room mantel. Inside was a letter from Brian telling me that he had taken the kids away because of all the negative influences now surrounding them. He referenced each member of my family in the most despicable of terms, and threatened to kill himself and the kids if I came looking for them. He warned me that he had friends in Detroit who would be keeping an eye on me and letting him know what I was up to.

I tore the letter to shreds and flushed it down the toilet. I felt I couldn't let any of my family-Mother in particular-see what he had written about them. But I did tell the police about it, especially the threats, but still to no avail.

But I was inspired by my dream. I felt I knew what I had to do, which was primarily keep my house and the kid's rooms in order until they got back. And keep looking for them.

I dropped out of school, got a job, joined the national organization then called Children's Rights, Inc. that's mission was the governmental adoption of legislation to stop child-snatching. I wrote to local leaders for help, and those at the federal level, the FBI and even Interpol but nobody could do anything for me. I called Brian's sister in England several times to the point where I think she got annoyed with me. And each time I talked to her she told she hadn't heard anything from her brother, but promised she would contact me if ever she did. I called Monica Barrett. She had been my best friend in Liverpool and was always comforting and supportive. I tried tracking down some of Brian's old friends and buddies but only one, Michael Burgess, whose nick name was Wally, empathized with me. In fact, he did more than that. He told me that Brian had been acting very strange before I even left him; that he thought Brian had, "*…gone 'round the bend,*" and he urged me to keep looking and get the kids away from him. He promised me that he would do whatever he could to help me, and he did. When he got wind that Brian had been seen back in New York, he both called and wrote to me to let me know.

I went back to New York looking for them, to the Haymarket, the Seaton, anyplace I could think of where they may have been.

It was like looking for a needle in a haystack and proved futile in the end.

I talked to private detectives, all of whom wanted big bucks I didn't have just to start an investigation. But one of them told me, after listening to my endeavors so far, that he would only be doing what I had already done and to keep my money. He said he was a former cop and that, based on his experience and what I'd told him about my ex, just to sit tight and wait for Brian to resurface. He said Brian fit the profile of a certain type of individual whose real objective was to hurt me the only way he knew he knew how, by taking the children. A lot of that was based on Brian's letters.

There had been a series of them, all of them with a local postmark, and all of them menacing in one way or another. But Brian warned me not to be fooled by the postmark. He wrote that he was miles away and was sending these letters to a friend of his in Detroit who would then post them to me. He also said that this friend was keeping tabs on me and that Brian knew everything I was up to. It was eerie to think I was being watched that way.

The letters also talked about the new religious salvation he had found and that he could help me find it too. He still spoke ill of my family but not as harshly as previously. And he still threatened to kill himself and the kids if I came after him.

Time marched on, weeks and even months, and the letters kept coming. It was my faith and belief in that dream that kept me going. Some people thought I was nuts: my missing kids were all I talked about. Some family members and friends tried to get me to accept a reality that I'd never see them again, but I knew better.

I went back to school evenings, found a better paying job at Sentry Insurance as a receptionist, and made a new friend named Mary Ann Rodgers who would become indispensable in our lives.

She was a single mother too. The love of her life had been brutally killed but she stayed determined to make the best life possible for herself and their daughter. She had another younger daughter as well, and the love she exuberantly showered on both of them was contagious when beheld. At Sentry, she was studying to become an agent but her ultimate goal was to open her own hair care business in Ypsilanti which she did. When I left Sentry to take a state job working with children she and I stayed friends.

My job at the Plymouth Center was on the day shift starting at 6:00 a.m. My work there tied in with my psych studies at Wayne State from where a few us were recruited, including another woman, also named Karen, whose father was a cop willing to help me locate my kids. And in truth, I loved working with the center kids. They became sort of a substitute for my own two who were still missing.

One morning, as I arrived for work and got out of my car, I saw this incredible essence alight in the sky. I'd never seen anything like it before in my life. Although afar, and somewhat diffused, it was still brilliant. I didn't know what to make of it. I went inside and, before clocking in, I asked others what they thought of it. No one seemed to know what I was talking about. But I felt sure they must have seen it. It was too big to have been missed. I pressed them further; still, no one gave any credence to what I was saying, and when they started looking at me strangely, I dropped the subject and just got on with day's work.

The next morning, the same thing happened only the light was even more intense and I felt afraid. It was so otherworldly. I froze in my tracks as I looked up at it and started to quiver; then gradually, I backed my way to my building and inside the door. This time I only asked once and ever so softly if anyone had seen that light outside. With the eye rolls I got in response, I knew to let it go. But I was unnerved by the experience the rest of the day.

On the third day, I was apprehensive as I parked my car, but once outside, the light seemed to gently envelope my spirit. I was not afraid, I was comforted by it. There was a mystical quality to it. There was no voice or words spoken aloud; still, I got a clear message not to worry and that everything was going to be alright. I walked into work calmly with my head held high, said my good-mornings, and went about my day. I didn't ask anybody anything about the light. I knew what I had seen and experienced and felt exceptionally good about it.

As I left work that afternoon, I followed my usual routine and went home, changed clothes, grabbed a quick study and some food, and headed down to Wayne for school. I had a big exam that evening. I had just gotten off the Lodge freeway and almost to campus grounds when. . . .

I opened my eye and stared into more bright lights, and there were muffled voices surrounding me asking if I could hear them. I tried to look around but my head wouldn't move nor would any of the rest of my body.

"Lay still," one of the voices said. "You're in the hospital, the emergency room. You've been in an accident and you're hurt on the outside, and we need to look inside you to make sure you're okay on the inside. Will you give us permission to do that?"

No words would come out of my mouth.

Another voice explained, "We need to do a laparoscopy where we'll make a tiny incision in your tummy and insert a little camera that will look around and show us if you have any internal bleeding."

Someone else offered, "She can't talk."

"Blink your eyes if it's okay," came an offside suggestion.

I blinked.

Another someone held a clipboard in front of my face and said, "I'll need you to sign this paper giving us permission to do the procedure." Then yet another someone place a pen between my fingers and guided them into making an "X" on the requisite line.

When I woke up again I was in a hospital room in traction. Everything was hazy. I still didn't know what had happened. One of the nurses told me the good news that I had no internal bleeding, it was all on the outside. I'd been hit in a high-speed police chase, and the car they were after was going 75 mph when it plowed into my little Ford Falcon that was now in two pieces, and I was lucky to be alive.

I couldn't move my body. Parts of me were strung up while other parts were strapped tight, wired together, or encased in a metal contraption.

Mother came to see me. I knew I must have looked bad by the expression on her face as she talked to me. My cop friend came too and kept trying to persuade me to let him call Brian's sister in England and tell her about the accident. I said no, of course, because I saw no point to it. But he kept insisting that *blood is thicker than water* and eventually I gave in. My father dropped by briefly and, fortunately, was there when the two officers who had done the chasing also stopped in. I misread their intentions at first and thought that they were genuinely concerned about my wellbeing. But when their questioning turned to what kind of music I liked, and what was I listening to in the car, and how loud it might have been I grew suspicious. Mary Ann would have seen through their questioning immediately as she did when I told her about it. But at the time, I had bigger concerns on my mind.

Several different doctors did their rounds with me. One explained that the broken glass from my windshield had just barely missed my jugular but that he would be able to redirect the scar left on my neck with plastic surgery. Another explained that my knee had been busted when the steering wheel fell on it during the mayhem, and yet another assured me that the wiring on my face would eventually be removed and was only there because my jaw had been dislodged but would heal in time. As for my right arm, it was going to take a lot of hard work in physical therapy to get it moving again. I listened to all this and took it in slowly, but when the white coat that told me about my broken neck and damaged spine ended his spiel by saying I'd never walk again, I screamed at him, "You're a lie," and started yelling for someone to get me out of there.

I must have caused a stir because folks started coming in from all directions, and they were all talking fast and loud to one another but not to me. After they left, I started twisting my body this way and that way in an effort to get myself up and out. It didn't work, and I lay back exhausted. Eventually an afternoon clinician came in and, after examining me again, announced that I could start PT next week and I did.

By the time I was discharged, I was hobbling on crutches with my right arm in a sling, a brace on my right knee, and wearing a metal chest plate with upright extensions surrounding my neck to keep it in place. I was clumsy and awkward but feeling no pain thanks to all the medication I was on.

Mary Ann helped me at home. She put me to bed, called often to check on me, stopped in routinely with soups and other soft foods and made arrangements for a visiting nurse to come by. Nita and Mother took turns picking me up for Physical Therapy where I still had to go three times a week. It was exhausting for everyone but I was determined to make progress and I did.

Then one evening, after answering the phone, I froze where I lay as I heard Brian's voice on the other end of the line. While he expressed sympathy for my predicament, I realized at once that my cop friend had been right. The only way he could have known about my situation was if Vera had told him. I asked about the kids and to speak with them but he wouldn't let me. He told me they were fine and that they did missed me. He also told me that the accident was the wrath of God and my punishment for filing for divorce from him, but that I could earn forgiveness (whether from him or from God I was never sure)if I sold the house and brought him the money and that way we could all be reunited.

Of course I said that I would.

He said that he'd call me back tomorrow, and that I shouldn't tell anyone that I had heard from him.

It took several more conversations and me lying my head off before Brian let me talk to the kids, and then it was ever so briefly. I just needed to hear their voices and to know that they were alright.

All my family was aghast. My father, who at that time was in the real estate business, researched the market value of the house so I could tell Brian that I'd put it up for sale and at what price the next time he called. And I did.

The next time I talked to Brian, I told him that I had a buyer for the place and a deposit. He was pleased, and said I should send him that money. I agreed and asked for his address. Surprisingly, he gave it to me.

When my father found out that Brian was in California his immediate reaction was to call Sandy, his sister Joann's son.

As the story goes, Edward Lindsey, Jr. had light brown hair when he was a little boy which was how he acquired the nickname *Sandy*. Since then, however, he'd grown up and become a career cop with the LAPD rising to the rank of Detective. And he was badass.

Dad got him on the phone and brought him up to date.

As for me, now that I knew where the kids were, I was ready to go get them. Sandy said he'd pick me up at LAX the next day.

But the next morning when I awoke, I noticed a white, sticky substance on my pillow and more of the same on the back of my head. Mary Ann said that it looked infected and took me the ER.

Being back there was like déjà vu, and I remain convinced to this day that the doctor who saw me then was the same one who cared for me right after the accident. I can recall a moment when, still on the gurney, my eyes moved sideways and saw him moving away, using a cane, and it occurred to me that he had been so gentile with me because he himself had once been hurt.

The doctor concurred that my head was infected as a result of never having been turned when I was in traction. He wrote orders to have me readmitted. But I explained that I couldn’t do that. I talked on and on- the whole story about the kids being snatched and now I’d found them. I told him that I had a plane ticket in my purse for an afternoon flight and a friend waiting outside to take me to Metro.

The man listened to me. He actually listened.

Then he told me that the infection was traveling inward toward my brain and that if it got there I’d be a vegetable. He said he’d do surgery right there, on the spot, and scoop out the poison but that I'd have to clean it every two hours with peroxide and rewrap it with clean gauze and take this strong antibiotic that he was prescribing. I agreed, he worked his magic, and then he told me to go get my kids.

Sandy met me at the airport and took me to Aunt Joann's.
He laid out the plan. Brian and the kids were in Pomona, which was out of his jurisdiction but just a train ride away. We would go there the next day and stay with Aunt Joann's other brother, Uncle Elijah, Elijah Ambrose, who was usually referred to as E.A. He and his wife Martha lived in a beautiful home in Ganesha Park.

Once we got there, after all the male backslapping and another rewrap of my head, Sandy was off to rally support from the local police. When he came back, he announced that our caper would commence in the early morning hours: the element of surprise was what he was after, and but for one minor miscalculation it should have worked.

It was shortly after 2:00 a.m. and we were all sitting around the kitchen table when Sandy announced it was time to go. E.A. drove us to the police station where I was ushered into the back seat of one squad car while Sandy called up and took charge of three others. He told me to sit tight and keep quiet until we got the kids.

The convoy cruised into a quiet neighborhood and surrounded a small framed house. Sandy barreled his way up to the front door while the uniformed officers positioned themselves at side and back entrances. Sandy knocked on the door. There was no answer. He rang the doorbell, knocked again, then banged. Neighbor's lights came on. He shouted an authoritative command. More lights but still no answer. After another moment or two and conferring with his crew, he came over to me and leaned his head inside the car window and whispered, "Looks like nobody's home." Then he asked me, "Any idea where they might be?" How would I know?

We went back to Uncle Elijah's. Sandy wanted to come up with another plan but all I kept thinking about was the neighbor's lights, and that they'd tell Brian what had happened, and that he'd know I had been out there, and that I needed to get back to Michigan. Brian had been calling me regularly and if he called and I wasn't home, he'd know for sure that I'd been out there.

The next morning I was on a return flight back to Detroit. No sooner than

I was back on Prevost, Brian called again. He said he'd been trying to get hold of me and wanted to know where I'd been. I told him about my head being infected and that I had been readmitted into the hospital and only just released. He bought it. He let me talk to the kids. He asked me when the money would be coming. I told him that just as soon as the buyer's check cleared the bank I'd send it on.

My father would come by my house often, get Sandy on the phone, and the two of them would strategize. "You just leave this to Sandy," dad would say to me. "He knows what he's doing."

Maybe he did, but now that I knew where the kids were, I was too antsy to just sit around and wait. Besides, the men began to cut me out of the whole equation like I was just window dressing. Several months after Brian had taken the kids, Mother and I befriended a cyclist named Walter Johnson that we met walking around Belle Isle. He was also a photographer and took several pictures of us. Over the months that followed, he became a good friend. He was also an interesting character.

Walt rode a titanium bike that cost three times as much as any of his cars and he only drove MGBs-albeit second or third hand models-that he kept operational on a rotating repairing system. He was tall and skinny with a complexion the color of coal and, when he wasn't shooting and developing his own pictures, he practiced the art of calligraphy. He was just a few years older than me and confessed a few times that, growing up in Ohio, he never expected to live to see age of eighteen. That's how rough it was where he was from. He credited his mother for his longevity.

When I first knew him, he was working in one of the auto plants in what was supposed to be a dream job: to push a button every fifteen minutes on the fifteenth minute. Easy peasy, but he couldn't stand it. What was he supposed to do those other fourteen minutes? He'd talk on the phone, socialize, read a book or a newspaper, get caught up and miss his quarter mark. And then there'd be hell to pay. He kept trying for the sake of his friend who had gotten him the job but in the end he quit and went back to school.

Before the plant he had been substitute teaching but found the kids too disrespectful. When he went back to school to pursue his Masters it would be in Computer Programming; eventually he would work for the IRS.

Walt was a good listener and, unlike many others in the community, he never condemned me for having married a white man. He understood my angst and anxiety over Brian having the kids and was always supportive of anything I did to find them. So as days went on, and my father and Sandy continued to entertain their various schemes and game plans without me, and dismissed my growing exasperation, I called Walt and asked him to take me to the airport. He said he'd be there in fifteen minutes and he was.

"Where you goin' girl?" my dad asked me when he saw me headed for the front door.

"I'm going to go get my kids." I told him.

"You ain't going nowhere," he said, and then added, "Sandy's takin' care of this. You better come back here and sit down."

Walt honked a second time and I hobbled out the door.

Still wearing a metal neck brace and with gaze bandages around my head, my right arm in a sling, and my right knee securely compressed to keep it from buckling, Walt folded me into his roadster and took off.

This time I flew into Ontario Airport and, with only twenty-three dollars left to my name, I climbed into a taxi and told the driver to take me as close to Pomona Police Station as that amount of money would get me. It must have been close to 3:00 a.m. when we got there.

The desk sergeant on duty didn't know what to say to me after his initial greeting of, "May I help you?"

My response was a resounding yes as I pulled out the volumes of documentation that I had brought with me from Detroit. I laid it all out and began my litany of the whys and wherefores of my case, and concluded it with, "I need you to help me find my kids."

The poor, young fellow looked stunned. "There's nothing I can do," he finally said. "You'll have to come back during the day shift."

I gathered up all my paperwork and sat down.

"You can't stay here," he said once he realized my intention.

"I just flew in here, I have two dollars left and no place to go," I informed him. "If I have to wait till the day shift, I'll wait here."

"You can't," he protested. "I can arrest you for loitering."

"Either way," I said, "I'll still be right here till the next shift" and with that, I bought a cup of coffee from their vending machine and moved to the back of the lobby where I sat another four or five hours.

As morning crew members started to arrive I went through the same scenario with each one who asked to help me, only it became a matter of having to wait for their Chief to come on duty.

When he arrived, I watched him huddle with one officer after another and look my way several times before disappearing into a back office.

I drank more coffee to stay awake and waited.

At long last I was called back.

The Chief listened to my story, seemed to size me up, and made a series of phone calls both local and out-of-state before asking me to wait again out in the lobby.

Finally he came out and told two of his underlings that I needed to be taken to a different precinct where they would be able to help me.

Once we got there, I recited my story a few more time until I was ushered into a private sitting room. After a while, I was told I needed to go to the Marshal's Office and I was driven there where a very polished young man talked way over my head about this case law and several others. Eventually I accompanied him into a law library where he told me what volume number he wanted me to help him look for. I found it. He read through it, smiled broadly, and sent me back to the precinct.

Another half hour or so there, then officers came and got me again.

"Where are we going this time?" I asked.

"We're going to get your kids," came the reply.

I sat stunned in the back seat of a squad car once again, and listened to the explanations being given to me. They had found Michelle by going through the public school's data base, but they had not been able to locate Daniel. Everything had taken so long because they'd first had to check me out thoroughly: my legal papers, background; they'd had to talk to my lawyers; check state statues.

Suddenly I was nervous, and keenly aware of how awful I must have looked. I reached into my bag and pulled out the Barbie and Big Truck I'd brought with me. I wished I could take a shower.

We pulled up in front of the Roosevelt School and one of the officers went inside to talk to school officials before I was brought into the building. Then I was told that the police needed to speak to Michelle first before I would be allowed to see her. I sat, and waited. Finally I saw her in the distance, and I heard the officer ask her if she knew who I was. She smiled said, "That's my mommy," and came rushing toward me. After a few hugs and kisses, the cops pulled us outside and explained that the Principal hadn't been pleased about our showing up and, by now, was probably on the phone to Michelle's father.

They asked Michelle if she wanted to come with me and when she replied in the affirmative, they told her that they hadn't been able to locate her brother and asked if she knew where he was. She said he went to the Christian Lifebuilders School and we went there.

I could see that he was a little apprehensive as he came out but he followed Michelle's lead and joined us in the squad car. We drove to Brian's house, the same place where that infamous, late-night fiasco had taken place.

"Is there anything inside that you want to get? Clothes? Toys?" Michelle answered for the both of them. "All our clothes are old," she said, "the same ones we were wearing in Detroit, but we do need to get Danny's medicine."

The cops asked, "Do you have a key to get in?"

Michelle said no.

"We can't go inside because it would be considered breaking and entering. . ."

Michelle interrupted, "The kitchen window is unlocked, and the medicine is on the window seal."

We all moved around to the side of the house but the bottled liquid wasn't within an arm-stretched reach.

"Listen," the cop said to Michelle, "if I left you up, you think you can get in there and get that medicine and anything else you might want?"

"Sure," she said. And with that she was hoisted up and in with a warning to hurry because Brian was probably on his way.

A few moments later we were back in the cop's vehicle and zooming back to their precinct. Once inside, the desk sergeant asked if we had any place to stay.

"My plan," I said, "was to get us back to Detroit as soon as possible."

"Not now," the desk cop explained. "Your ex just called here to complain that we had helped you steal your kids and he wants them back. I told him it was too late, that we had just driven you out to the airport. He's on his way there now."

I immediately got in touch with Uncle Elijah who said of course we could stay with him, but he was the only one on duty at the store at the moment and could the cops bring us there.

They agreed and drove us to the Ferguson-Pac-A-Bag store that was just three blocks away from where the kids had been living. In fact, the kids had been in there before, and had seen Uncle Elijah and remarked to each other how much he reminded them of their grandfather back in Detroit.

All those Ferguson boys look alike.

Uncle Elijah and his wife Martha opened their hearts and home to us; still, I was anxious to get back home, but I had wiped out my bank account getting out there. I called my father and asked him, if I wrote a check to the airline to get home, would he put the money in my account? He reluctantly agreed.

The kids ran straight to their old rooms as soon as we got back on Prevost and were surprised to see them as they remembered. I ran up my charge accounts re-outfitting them but was delighted to see them so happy. I wasn't sure what was going to happen next, and I figured Brian would cause a stir, but nothing prepared me for the crucible to come or the ordeals we were yet to encounter.

Mixed Blessings

Folks came from out of the woodwork to welcome the kids back home. It had been a year and a half since they had been taken and most had given up hope that I would ever see them again and urged me to do the same. Get on with your own life, some told me, while others suggested that I look at the situation realistically: He's white, he can go anywhere. What you gonna do? But now that they were back, all that cautioning was forgotten. I was praised for my tenacity and for having kept the faith.

Physically I got better every day, and I credit the kids as being motivational factors. My head healed, my knee got stronger, and my neck was upgraded into a soft collar. I still went to therapy to increase the range-of-motion of my right arm, which still hurt, but rarely did I use a sling anymore.

My visiting nurse was discharged, but Mary Ann was always there and picked up any slack. She was my best friend and we planned our respective futures together. She had already quit the insurance company and opened her own business in Ypsi; and, while I was still on a medical disability from my state job, and I knew it wouldn't last forever, I used that time off to re-connect with my children and, in the process, learned a lot about what had gone on while they were away.

It turned out that Adrian, Vera's oldest son, had come over from England to help Brian execute his plan; that they had driven from Detroit to Texas to California, then flown back to England, then back to California before I found them. Initially Brian had told the children that I would be joining them, but when I didn't show up, he said that I mustn't love them anymore. Brian had become "*born again*" and was fond of quoting the bible passage that read, "*spare the rod, and spoil the child*" and used a belt to keep the kids in line.

Since Danny was now of school age, I enrolled them both in St. Mary's of Redford which was in walking distance of our house. I took them there in the morning and picked them up when school was out. And the nuns, teachers and priest there all knew of our situation and formed a protective arch over them.

People kept saying I should sue the police for engaging in that high-speed chase; especially since, as I learned, it was a silent run; they were in pursuit for a moving violation that had gone from Grosse Pointe through downtown and up near Wayne State during rush hour; the perpetrators they were after had skipped out on their bail and skipped town; and all the while they were chasing there was aerial surveillance of the car which meant that the chase was unnecessary.

I did seek legal counsel about it but, from my perspective, that accident was what lead to me finding the kids and was therefore remained a blessing in disguise. So the motions I went through in that regard were secondary to getting the kid's lives back on track, and there was still a lot to do.

After my disability ran out, the State informed me that I would not be allowed to come back to work in my former capacity because I was now considered a liability. The children I worked with there did act out, and I had been attacked a couple times, so to bring me back in direct care of such youngsters was considered just too risky. There was no other position there for which I was qualified so I had to find a less demanding job elsewhere myself.

There were two Help Wanted Ads in the newspaper that had been placed by Kingswood Hospital. I applied for them both, didn't get the first but was hired for the second, a mid-afternoon shift in Admitting. And so began my career in hospital administration that would last some thirteen years.

I would walk the kids to school in the morning then take three buses to work. After school, the kids would stay with their nearby babysitter, Mrs. Bridges, until I picked them up. Then we'd all walk back home together, have dinner, romp and get ready for bed.

HILDA LOUISE BRIDGES

My sister Anita-Maria(a.k.a. Sam)

Mary Ann Rodgers

Ernestine & Me Mother

An outing with Walter →

And Reunion with

← Mary Ann

One Conundrum After Another

The knock on the front door was so gentle that I was barely sure I'd heard it. It was a Saturday. The kids were watching TV. Was that a knock? I asked myself, then went to check to make sure. I looked out the peep hole and sure enough, there stood Brian.

The screen door was locked so I opened the front door just enough for him to see my newfound, hardcore stance. "Go away," I told him. "You're no longer welcome here."

"I want to see the kids," was all he said at first.

"No," I said.

"Danny, Michelle, Daddy's here," he began shouting, and the kids poked their heads around when they heard the commotion.

"Go upstairs," I told them and they did.

"I trusted you once," I said to him, "but never, ever again."

"I'm their father. I've got my rights. I just want to see them, that's all" was what he came back with.

"You violated any rights you had when you took them," I said just before closing the door.

But that was only the first of several assaults he made on our humble abode. He would show up late afternoons or at dusk and shout up to the kid's bedroom windows how much he loved them. Or he'd march up and down in front of the house with picket signs that read, "Mom won't let dad see kids." He posted notes on the front door in our absence. There were phone calls when no one spoke if I answered. Then in one shouting match when he threatened to stick the law on me, feeling assured of my own righteousness, my finals words to him were, "I'll see you in court," and I did.

My father's lawyer friend was no longer interested in representing me because, as he said, "There's no money in this case." So he assigned it to one of his associates, Timothy Yockey. He was young and ponytailed, smart, and wanting to see justice in the world. But even he warned me that, at some point, I would have to allow Brian "reasonable" visitation.

But no visitation was reasonable to me, not after what he had done.

I kept moving forward. I bought another secondhand car and worked hard on my anxieties of getting behind the wheel again. It was hard for me. I'd pull up at a street light or stop sign and sit there endlessly, looking both ways repeatedly, before inching forward on the road. It took even longer for me to drive on the freeway. I was terrified of being blindsided again.

There was a lull before the first storm hit.

Weeks had gone by with no sighting of Brian and then Tim Yockey called with a court date. But Brian wasn't just seeking visitation, he wanted full custody of the kids.

"What!" I was flabbergasted.

His argument was that he had taken good care of the kids the year and a half that he had had them so he should be allowed to continue to do so.

I thought it was all so preposterous and argued back that he had previously stolen the kids in violation of a court decree that had given temporary custody to me; that he was in this country illegally and had already taken the kids out of the country and was likely to do so again; that he had been abusive to me and to the kids and was trying to force his newfound religion on them instead of the one we had previously agreed upon and had the kids baptized in; and he wasn't contributing anything financially to the kid's well-being.

It didn't matter. A custody trial was ordered. It lasted for five days in the courtroom of Judge Myron H. Wahls who, at one point looked up over his readers and said, "I've heard this story before."

When it was over, I retained custody but was ordered to allow visitation.

Brian filed an appeal.

By the time of the second trial, which took just as long as the first and was based on some procedural technicality, my nerves were on edge and my lawyer was asking for money.

I had no savings. The only thing I had of value was the house in which we were living. My father shrugged but then came up with a buyer while Uncle Bobby scoffed and groused. "You know you don't have to put up with none of this," he said, "a ninety-nine cent jug of wine can take care of a whole lot of business."

It was while I was looking for a new place that I ran into Warren Garner, a local realtor, who said I reminded him of his daughter. We got to talking and I spewed out my situation with the kids as I still had a tendency to do. He looked at me in amazement and said he'd tell his wife about it and maybe she would write about it in the paper. His wife, it turned out, was June Brown, a columnist then for the Detroit News. And sure enough, she did give me a bit of coverage in the press.

12-B—THE DETROIT NEWS

It's the child who loses in custody, support cases

June Brown

Some of the most ignored human tragedies occur in child custody and child support cases. The saddest part is that the public is either reluctant to interfere or tries to ignore the whole thing.

The courts need to establish guidelines for child custody cases. Should fathers get custody of sons and mothers get custody of daughters? Should a mother who abandoned a child be given custody again?

Parents in recent cases have been pouring out their problems to me. In one case, Karen, a black woman, married a white man but when marital problems began, she divorced him and took the two children with her. He begged her to come back but she refused. When he discovered he couldn't get her back, he sued for custody of the children. He makes more money than she does and can hire a good lawyer. The case has not been heard and she still has her children. But the fear of losing her children is devastating her emotionally.

ON THE OTHER hand, Gary has cared for his 3-year-old son since he was 4 months old. Gary and his son's mother weren't married but Gary signed papers establishing paternity and giving the child his name. The child's mother did not want the boy and, according to Gary, she would not even take him to the hospital when he was sick.

Now that she is pregnant again, she wants her son back because her ADC check will be larger if she has two children, Gary said.

When Gary wouldn't surrender custody of the child, the police went to Gary's church, took his son out of his arms and gave him back to the woman who had deserted him.

Gary, who works on a low-salaried job, rushed to Legal Aid and asked them to represent him. Legal Aid refused but, because the mother receives ADC, the agency agreed to represent her.

Now the mother has her son, a larger ADC check and a free lawyer furnished by Legal Aid. All Gary has is memories.

JOYCE, WHO has been divorced nine years, has never collected the $15 weekly support for two children, which the court ordered.

Her husband spent eight years in prison where he earned two associate degrees. Now that he's out of prison, he won't work. Joyce told me that he was offered a job but turned it down because he got a grant and can go to school free.

At present, he is living free on the campus of a large university, receiving a monthly allowance and free medical care while she struggles to pay for her family's health care on her small salary. The government takes care of the father but the children get nothing.

Shirley's husband was in the Navy but is out now, living on an ample pension. She and her children get none of his pension money, although they are having extreme financial difficulty. She works for a large utility company that has been kind enough to give her a low-interest loan to help her out.

AND THE SAD stories go on.

The biggest difficulty with these cases is that no one knows which parent is lying and which is telling the truth. But, for the children's sake, the public must take more interest in custody cases and find solutions that are fair.

The house I found was at 19384 Telegraph and I took the kids with me to see it when I went to meet with the owner, Al Dubay. They picked out their bedrooms right away. It was a cute, little ranch with a full basement, screened-in back porch, big back yard and garage. It seemed perfect but I couldn't afford it. Then for whatever reason-maybe he was charmed by the kids-Al Dubay came down on the rent. I still felt I couldn't afford it but he said, "You will, if you want it," and I did for the next seven years.

I had actually started providing visitation before we ever moved to Telegraph Road. Yockey had gotten it stipulated that the visits were to be weekends, in my home, and supervised by me. That left me in a quandary. I worked all week and couldn't enjoy the weekends with my kids. And being stuck in my own home with Brian was excruciating for me. But he was the one who complained. He said I was spying on him.

Spying on him?! Of course I kept watch on him: the visits were being supervised. And I did object to the constant praying he did with and over the kids, and the fact that he wouldn't listen to me. Any request I made or conversation I tried to have with him was met with a religious rejoinder. "Praise the Lord," he'd suddenly shout or, "God forgive her," or some Bible quotation. It was maddening, and the visits were long, two or three hours each day.

In truth, there were times when I just couldn't take it and I took the kids out rather than have them cooped up in the house, like when the Ice Capades came to town. We had a ball, but then I was show-caused (i.e. hauled into court to show cause why I shouldn't held in contempt for not following a court order). I explained that my children were being deprived of so much of life's enjoyment. I was chastised and warned not to do it again.

Visitation on Telegraph Road went more smoothly at least during the warm weather months when much of it took place outside in the back yard. But then one day my next door neighbor came to see me because he'd found packets of poison in his yard undoubtedly put there for his dog. He knew my kids loved his dog. They played with him through the neighboring fence. He also said that he had a good idea of who had placed those packets there. I knew too, but there was nothing I could do or say about it. I couldn't prove it.

In court, Brian kept asking for more and more visitation. And he continuously complained that I was somehow interfering with the time he did have. It wasn't true. While it had been true in the past that I had not always complied, I was starting to see the pattern that was developing here. Gradually more and more time was being given to Brian and eventually he would ask for visitation away from the home.

And it wasn't just the pattern, he would tell me so. In court corridors he'd sometimes saddle up to me and whisper things in my ear to suggest that he was going to win in the end or that I was going to get mine. And he'd bring his latest white girlfriend with him for whatever purpose she was meant to serve. It was all so subtle and yet obvious. Still, nothing prepared me for that day I was ordered to report to court with no specific objective stated. It wasn't another show-cause hearing, no motions had been filed that my attorney was aware of, I hadn't asked for more in child support because I'd already learned that was a waste of time. So what was it? Yockey and I would find out together.

There was a new kind of tension filling the air as we walked in for that next tribunal. Judge Wahls was mad, he was fuming. But Brian was sitting there with a smirk on his face. As the situation unfolded I learned that Brian had filed charges against Judge Wahls with the Judicial Tenure Commission. Because I had not been punished as a result of any of my show-cause hearings, Brian claimed that the judge was biased in my favor; and, while an investigation was pending, the Judge Wahls could not hear cases.

He slammed down a gavel then pointed at me and said that to prove that he was not biased, I was to be locked up for a week in jail.

What?!

I was stunned. My lawyer was horrified. Then the bailiffs came and hauled me off to the bullpen. "But I've been letting him visit," I managed to blurt out as I was being taken away, but nobody seemed to hear me.

My lawyer did come to see me as I was literally sitting there behind bars awaiting the van that would take me to jail. "Write a letter of apology to the judge," he told me.

"No!" I shouted back to him. It was clear to me that this whole episode had now devolved into a cock fight between Brian and Judge Wahls, and none of it had anything to do with either me or the well-being of the kids.

I served my time. My one phone call was to Mary Ann with requests that she keep the kids in my absence and call my boss at work to let her know what had happened.

After I got out, I found out that Brian had gone to Mary Ann's house and tried to get the kids from her but she was to savvy to let that occur. I also found out that, while I was in, Brian had also tried to appeal to the courts for custody once again. His claim was that I must be an unfit mother otherwise I wouldn't be locked up in jail. Thankfully, that didn't fly either.

From that day on, every time I had to appear in court I had a packed bags with me. My attitude was, if I'm locked up again at least I'll be comfortable. I just hadn't expected it to come when Wahls was off the bench.

He was having his bunions operated on and a visiting judge was handling his docket who was unfamiliar with the dynamics of our case. So when Brian got in front of him and started lying about this, that and the other, I just couldn't keep my mouth shut. The judge told me to be quiet and I guess I should have but I just couldn't, not even when I heard him say, "One more word, I'll hold you in contempt. . ."

So again came the bailiffs, and again I was shuttled off to the bullpen. This time, however, my lawyer had already apologized to the judge on my behalf before he ever came to see me and with release papers: a good thing I can say with hindsight, but at the time I was mad. How dare he, I thought, and that was the final nail in that coffin.

A week or so later, I called the Women's League of Justice and got a list of referrals for other attorneys. I selected Katherine Barnhart; I'm not sure why, but she ended up being in direct contrast to Ruth Acevedo, Brian's crass, pixie, bottle-red bulldog of a barrister.

Katherine stood tall, and slim, and was always classically and elegantly appareled. She and her law partners had recently refurbished the historic Parker House at 975 East Jefferson and set up their practice there. It, too, was a direct reflection of her personality and style.

She listened to me, and really heard what was on my mind. As a woman and a mother, I believe she understood both my fears and frustration; as a good lawyer, she questioned any retaliatory act I entertained by asking, ". . . and what good will come of that?"

It was Katherine who also first questioned how Brian was able to afford Acevedo's services especially, since he had claimed so many times in court, he only earned a paltry wages working in food service as he did.

The answer came in the most astonishing way: Fr. Edward Haggerty, one of the priest at St. Mary's who was supportive of me and the kids, told me that one of the nuns had seen an article about Brian on the front page of the L.A. Times when she had been in California recently for a retreat.

It was hard for me to believe; my curiosity got the better of me. One night, when the kids were in bed, I call the news desk at the L.A. Times. The young lady who answered the phone there asked me details about the story I was trying to research but I didn't have many, only that it was about Brian and the kids. I couldn't even tell her the date the story ran. She said she'd try to see what she could find but I could tell from her voice it wasn't hopeful. Then she asked for an address where she could a copy if she found one.

When I told her Telegraph Road in Detroit, Michigan, she got excited. "I used to live on Telegraph Road when I was there in Michigan too," she said.

But not in Detroit, out Pontiac way, but there was an immediate bonding between us. And sure enough, not only did she find the original story and send me a copy of that but also a follow-up piece that also ran.

The headline read: "Father Seeking $954,000 in Custody Fight" and was followed-up on page 7 with a photo of Brian and the kids.

That realization prompted me to seek retribution for that high-speed chase, and I signed a promissory note to Katherine for whatever I might be awarded from a law suit I planned against the state police. But it was all for naught. There was a trial up in Lansing that I both lost and for which I was ordered to pay cost.

Los Angeles Times

March 25, 1981

Dear Mrs. Minard:

Enclosed is a copy of the Los Angeles Times article you were seeking. We are pleased to have been of assistance.

Sincerely,

Debi Ryono
Public Information Service

P.S. I lived off Telegraph in Monroe.

TIMES MIRROR SQUARE / LOS ANGELES, CALIFORNIA 90053 / TELEPHONE (213) 972-5000

Father Seeking $954,000 in Custody Fight

SAG DEC 2 7 1979

By MARK LANDSBAUM
Times Staff Writer

POMONA—H. Brian Minard stole his children, then so did his wife, he claims. And Minard, a 42-year-old former cab driver, bartender and songwriter, believes it has caused him nearly a million dollars in grief.

He is seeking $954,000 in damages from the City of Pomona, its school district and the county. 7-1-1

Minard prepared his children for the journey for two months. The three of them planned it secretly, he said. Even 3-year-old Danny did not mention a word of their plans to his mother.

On Feb. 10, 1978, Minard picked up his children from the Detroit, Mich., home of his estranged wife who was suing him for divorce, packed them and a few belongings into a borrowed car and drove to Pomona, to make a new life. He did not tell his wife they were leaving or where they intended to go.

"We lived happily ever after for 19 months," Minard recalled.

Minard, who worked as a window washer in Pomona, said he had become concerned when he heard from friends in Detroit that his wife had been in an auto accident. He telephoned her, but at first refused to let her know where he and the children were living.

A few conversations later, Minard said his wife convinced him that she wanted to become a born-again Christian like him and "live with us and see her kids grow up." He told her where they lived.

The children—9-year-old Michelle and Danny, now 5,—still did not want to see their mother, Minard said, nevertheless they prayed together that the family could be reunited.

On Sept. 11, 1979 Karen Minard came to Pomona and went to the police. Minard said he was unaware that his wife had been granted the divorce and custody of the children in Michigan.

She presented copies of the Michigan court order to police and declared that her former husband was in contempt of court, Minard said.

Police officers accompanied Mrs. Minard first to Roosevelt School where they picked up Michelle, then to Life Builders Christian School where they picked up Danny, and finally to Minard's apartment, where, he claims, police "broke into my home" and gathered the children's clothes while he was away.

Minard has filed claims for more than $950,000 against the City of Pomona, the Pomona Unified School District and Los Angeles County, asserting that police improperly removed his children from school and handed them over to his former wife.

(A claim for damages must be filed

Please Turn to Page 7

FATHER SUES IN CUSTODY FIGHT

Continued from First Page

with public agencies before a lawsuit can be filed.)

"In spite of the fact that there are laws declaring how this situation should be handled, three Pomona police officers took it upon themselves to enforce these Michigan court orders," Minard's claim against the city says. 7-7-1

It was solely due to the participation of police that school officials released the children, Minard's Pomona attorney Patricia Hopkins said.

At Michelle's school, police said, the mother had a valid court order, and at Danny's school when police were asked for legal papers the officers said they did not need them, Hopkins said.

M[illegible] has returned to Michigan to [illegible], though a court [illegible] hits him from

mother while knowing Mr. Minard had been the sole parent enrolling Michelle over a year ago."

When police went to Roosevelt School they spoke only with a secretary, M. L. Hickson, and a typist-clerk, Marsha Graham. Hickson and Graham told The Times. Neither the principal nor another administrator was involved, they said.

"It was one of those days when everybody was gone," Graham said.

The school unsuccessfully attempted to contact Minard, Hickson said. There was nothing the school employees could do to prevent police and Mrs. Minard from removing Michelle from school, she said.

Police showed the secretary and typist-clerk no documents and cited no law to justify their involvement, Hickson said.

Police contend they were along only to "keep the peace."

"The district policy, as far as I know, is that we have no legal authority to restrain the child," Hickson school by a parent when there is a dispute over custody.

That policy states that only the "responsible parent or guardian" shall be permitted to take a child from school, said Bill Stlzner, supervisor of child welfare and attendance.

If a parent other than the one identified in school records as the "responsible" parent (in this case the father) attempts to take a child from campus, school officials are supposed to require documentation that the parent has legal custody, Stelzner said.

If there is a dispute over custody, advice from the school district's administration should be sought, he said.

"You can really get into hairy legal ground there," Stelzner said.

Hickson and Graham told The Times that they did not telephone the district office for advice.

Stelzner also said that such incidents should be handled by the principal or a certificated employee such as a dean or teacher, rather than

mother had police officers' involvement not lent legitimacy to her demand.

Minard's claim against the county alleges that the district attorney's office gave "false and poor advice" to police, who may not have acted at all without that advice.

Minard does not intend to file a lawsuit against Life Builders Christian School, a parochial school from which his son Danny was removed. Hopkins said.

Officials at that school were "influenced" in releasing the boy to police, because Roosevelt School had earlier released Michelle, Minard's claim says.

Minard's claims ask for $401,00[illegible] from the city, $201,500 from the school district and $351,500 from the county for damages resulting from false imprisonment, battery, trespass, alienation of affections, emotion[illegible]

My case, for reasons I never fully understood, was tied to another high-speed case in which it was ruled that victims were not allowed to sue the officers who made the decision to chase. And I always had mixed feelings about that.

While I truly believed that the officers in my case should not have chased given the time of day, the inciting offence, and the aerial surveillance they had; still, that accident had in fact been the catalyst for reuniting me with my kids and so, from that perspective, a blessing in disguise.

The whole thing was yet another conundrum to be faced that nearly broke me. With not enough money to meet the terms of a negotiated court cost payment agreement, I was then threatened with garnishment.

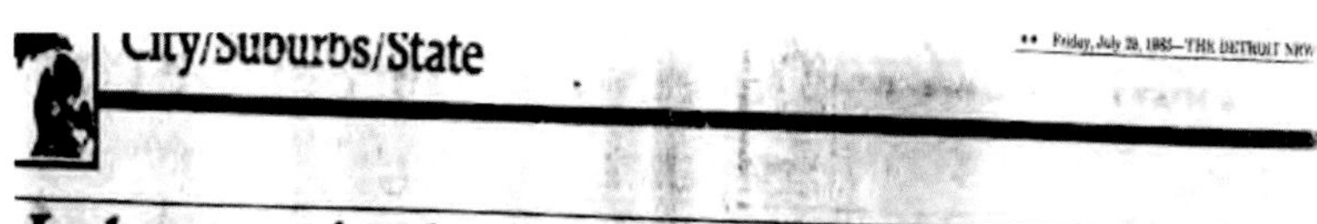

City/Suburbs/State

Friday, July 19, 1985—THE DETROIT NEWS

Judge won't charge deputy in 2-death chase

By Robert E. Roach
News Staff Writer

Angry Oakland County prosecutors accused a Pontiac judge of setting a "double standard" by refusing to sign a criminal warrant against a sheriff's deputy in the deaths of two men killed during a high-speed chase.

But District Judge Robert Cunningham's ruling yesterday drew applause from an overflow courtroom crowd of policemen, deputies and friends of Deputy Roger Geistler.

The ruling came one day after the Michigan Court of Appeals, in a similar case involving civil litigation, said state troopers could not be sued for their involvement in a police chase in which a woman was seriously injured.

IN THE OAKLAND County case, Chief Assistant Prosecutor Richard Thompson charged that yesterday's prewarrant hearing was "fixed from the beginning."

Thompson questioned the propriety of the unusual hearing, which was called to determine if there was enough evidence to sign the warrant. He accused the judge of using "one standard of justice for the common people, but a second standard for police officers."

Defense attorney Arthur Jay Weiss, of the Police Officers Association of Michigan, praised Cunningham's decision, saying that judges "aren't meant to be a rubber stamp for the prosecutor's office."

Prosecutor L. Brooks Patterson requested the warrant, which would have charged Geistler with negligent homicide in the 2 a.m. collision April 29. The offense is a high misdemeanor punishable by two years in jail.

PATTERSON SAID a three-month investigation determined that Geistler, an eight-year veteran, committed many violations of state law and his department's written "hot pursuit" policy when his squad car struck a vehicle not involved in the chase. The crash killed Jeffrey D. Nelson, 20, of Oxford, and Brian J. Wagner, 19, of Lake Orion.

The pursued car, which later proved to be stolen, was driven by another 19-year-old from Lake Orion. He is waiting trial for car theft.

According to testimony, the two victims in Nelson's subcompact were moving through a green light at Walton and Baldwin when Geistler ran the red light at nearly 80 mph.

Cunningham, however, relied on testimony that Nelson had a bad driving record and a "night vision" restriction on his license. When struck by the sheriff's car, testimony indicated, Nelson was legally intoxicated, had a beer bottle in his lap and his car radio was "blaring," the judge said.

THOMPSON SAID Cunningham's ruling may be appealed if prosecutors can show the judge's actions amounted to an "abuse of discretion."

The appellate ruling Wednesday held that Karen Minard, who was injured in Detroit on July 18, 1979, when her car was rammed by a driver being pursued by state police, may not sue the officers involved.

Ms. Minard's attorney, Morris Friedman, said he will seek to have the case consolidated with one [illegible] Ann Arbor already pending before state Supreme Court.

IN AFFIRMING dismissal of suit by the Michigan Court of Cla[illegible] the appeals court noted that dis[illegible]tionary actions of governm[illegible] officials — those involving indivi[illegible] judgment — are covered by the [illegible]munity shield.

"If any negligence on the par[illegible] the officers was a proximate caus[illegible] the injury to this plaintiff, it [illegible] negligence in the discretionary a[illegible] making the decision to chase (the [illegible]ing car), not negligence in the man[illegible] in which the police were driving t[illegible] vehicle," the court said.

United Press International cont[illegible]uted to this report.

And things kept getting worse from there.

During the time that charges were pending against Judge Wahls, Brian had picketed the City-County Building where the Judge's courtroom was housed. That attracted press coverage. He also joined forces with a group called Equal Rights for Fathers that provided him with a cadre of physical support the next few times that there were hearings. Some male members would march in like an army and make a real big noise in the process. From my perspective, our whole case was turning into a circus and taking a toll on the kids.

Michelle would stay in her room during visitations and Brian would blame that on me. And Danny, although he engaged with his father, was clearly torn by the loyalty he felt for both his parents. While I tried to be sympathetic to his feelings, Brian used them as springboards from which to fuel more atrocities on me. The incident that was most pronounced was when Brian gave Danny a pocket knife that I would not allow him to have.

I argued: He doesn't know how to use a knife like that but he is in Cub Scouts, so when he learns through that group then he can have it.

Brian quoted Bible passage after Bible passage and accused me of denying our son his father's love. He did take the knife back but then slipped it to Danny when I wasn't looking. And I ended up having to physically wrestle it away from him during a subsequent disagreement.

As time went on, and following court ordered psychiatric evaluations of both children, it was determined that Michelle was old enough-and mature enough-to have her opinion heard. She met with Judge Wahls alone in his chambers. Whatever was said during that meeting, only Michelle knows today as Judge Wahls took the contents of that conversation to the grave with him. But in the end it was concluded that Michelle no longer had to spend visitation time with her father.

There was more. One of the Court Clerks called me and said he'd like to help me with my case if only I'd meet him for dinner at the Red Lobster out on Southfield Rd. When I told Katherine about his invite, she had him removed from my case.

And then there was the time when, following a court hearing, as I walked with Katherine back to her office I realized that my car was no longer parked on Lafayette where I had left it. It had been stolen, and by the time it was found, it had been stripped and was beyond repair.

What else could possibly go wrong.

Although Judge Wahls was exonerated by the tribunal to which Brian had complained about him, and he was eventually appointed to the Michigan Supreme Court, Brian didn't stop. He continued to file motion after motion against me even listing the kids as plaintiffs, in one instance, with himself serving on their behalf as their "next friend."

Each motion sought more and more visitation, but the question became, to whose docket would our case be assigned now that Wahls had moved on. The answer: Paul Teranes, a tall, white, blind judge who was never without his seeing eye dog. Even during court room proceedings, it sat dutifully by his feet.

The issue of race had never been vocalized throughout any previous proceedings. Only once had I heard it referenced, and then it was from a black, female courtroom observer who thought I got what I deserved when I was threatened with contempt. "That's what she gets," the woman whooped, "for marrying a white man in the first place."

But the racial component was obvious. I was a black woman trying to free herself from the tyranny of a white man, and trying to use a system that had been designed for his benefit to do it. It didn't have to be discussed, it could clearly be seen.

By the time of our first appearance before Judge Teranes, Brian was on his own. A subsequent article had run in the L.A. Times saying that he had decided not to sue Pomona authorities after all. And so, with the loss of those lawsuits, so went the services of Ruth Acevedo.

In truth, Katherine Barnhart could have done the same with me but she didn't. And for that, I will always be grateful to her.

While he may have had some help drafting his legal briefs, Brian certainly filed them himself and made sure that I was served. And in court, representing himself, he was quite the spectacle as he strutted and pranced around in a baby blue, polyester suit, pontificating as if he was a student of the law and, furthermore, deserved an award for being Father of the Year.

Father Decides Not to Sue After Pomona Schools Turn Over Children to Ex-Wife

By MARK LANDSBAUM
Times Staff Writer

• POMONA—A former Pomona man has decided not to. sue city, school district and county officials after public' and private school officials turned over his children to his ex-wife 10months ago.

Brian Minard had filed $954,000 in claims against the: public agencies last December. However, attorney Patricia Hopkins said her client does not have the resources to pursue the lawsuits which, she said, inevitably would involve appeals to higher courts.

Minard, who moved to Detroit in December to be near, his children, had admitted secretly taking his son, Danny, 5, and daughter, Michelle, 9, from his estranged wife's Detroit home two and a half years ago.

After living in Pomona with the children for nearly two years, Minard said he learned that the children's mother, Karen Minard, had been in an auto accident. Minard said he telephoned her and she persuaded him to tell her where he and the children were living. He said' she did not mention that she had obtained a divorce.

In September, 1979, according to Minard's claim, his ex-wife showed Pomona police a Michigan court order, giving her custody of the children. Police accompanied Karen Minard to private and public schools here where she picked up the children.

Police then accompanied the three to Minard's home where, he claims, police "broke into my apartment" and, gathered the children's belongings. Minard said he discovered the children were gone when he arrived home from work.

Claims for damages were filed with the City of Pomona, the Pomona Unified School District and the County of Los Angeles, because police had acted on advice of 4 deputy district attorney, Hopkins said.

The officers acted wrongly because a Michigan order is not valid in California, the claim said.

For all police knew, Hopkins said, a subsequent court order which granted custody to the father could have existed.

Police should not have acted on the basis of the documents the mother showed them, Hopkins said. A

Instead, she said, Karen Minard should have used California civil courts to try to retrieve her children. .

The presence of police prompted school officials to turn over the children, Hopkins said.

She added that she felt that claims must be filed against all three public agencies. If not, she said, any agency served with a claim could place the blame on an agency which was not served.

Minard had lost a subsequent attempt in a Michigan court to gain custody of his children and was granted two hours of weekend visitation, Hopkins said.

His fight for custody in Michigan "was extremely hindered because all of his witnesses were in California," Hopkins said.

Because of the possibility of litigation, public school officials also refused to cooperate when asked to give written statements on Minard's behalf, Hopkins said.

"We've accomplished all that we are going to accomplish in preventing that from happening again," Hopkins said.

The Pomona Police Department has agreed to "educate" its officers on the proper procedure to follow under such circumstances, she said.

Minard is picketing the courtroom of the Michigan judge who he claims refused to enforce even his weekend visitation rights, Hopkins said.

I'd been on the stand before. When Ruth Acevedo had been pounding me, I'd given her back what she gave me with equal intensity. It hadn't served me well.

This time, as Brian came at me, reinforced with the Judge's insistence that I answer his questions, I broke down and cried. I don't remember exactly what the question was, or whether it was more the audacity of the situation, what I do remember is that afterwards even Katherine said my tears served to humanize me. It was as if, prior to that, my strength and resolve against Brian and the system were seen as negatives; still, to this day, I don't know any mother who would not have reacted similarly in my situation.

As sessions before Judge Teranes continued, it gradually became clear to Katherine that Brian was going to keep getting what he wanted which was visitation away from my home. But it was still a bombshell to me.

On April 1, 1986, Teranes ordered that Brian would have overnight visitation with Daniel on the third and fourth weekends of each month from 9:00 a.m. on Saturday to 5:00 p.m. on Sunday. And on those Sundays that weren't part of an overnight stay, Brian still had visitation with him from 12:30 to 6:30

away from my home. I felt like the inevitable April fool, but once the shock of it all dissipated, I resolved to make the situation work.

Brian and I had been married in 1969. Our divorce was finalized in 1978. We had been battling over the kids for another eight years. While time may not have healed all our wounds, the kids were older now, Michelle was thriving, and I had no desire to ever go back to jail. Furthermore, Mother was battling cancer and I wanted to spend more of my time with her. I made sure Danny knew how to get hold of me at all times, encouraged him to enjoy his time with his father, and prayed a lot all the time he was away from us.

Brian was living in Union Lake at the time, an Oakland County suburb nearly an hour's drive from Detroit. I couldn't help but steel myself every time he picked Dan up, and I never rested comfortably until he returned him to me.

Although Michelle had opted out of visitations, she and her brother remained close. One night, when Dan was out with his father in Union Lake, he called Michelle on the phone to tell her of his amazing discovery. He'd been walking around the subdivision in which Brain was living, and looked down at a stack of newspapers that a neighbor had bundled up and put out for refuse, and saw him and his sister's picture. It was the L.A. Times article.

Michelle didn't believe him at first and ran to ask me about it. When I confirmed the existence of the piece, and showed her my copy of that same story, she was upset that I hadn't ever told her about it before.

In truth, there was a lot I never told the kids about what was or had gone one during all this trauma. As I saw it then, it was my duty as a mother to protect them and provide them with an environment in which they would do well. I hid a lot from the-ugly details-and in the long run I still tend to think that was best.

But then one day when Brian showed up for visitation he had another surprise for me. Not only had he moved from Union Lake back to Detroit, he'd bought a house just a five minute drive from me at 18997 Westbrook. While Dan seemed delighted with the situation of being close to his mom and his dad, I shivered at the idea. I'd already known Brian skulked around my house at strange hours of the night as was evidenced by the notes I find on my door early mornings. Having him so close by was disarming to me. And how had he been able to buy a house anyway when in court he always pleaded broke.

But Dan remained thrilled and would want to go to Brian's house many times not ordained, and I could sense what was brewing.

Mother was living at the Farmington Nursing Home then but had to be hospitalized sometime in December during the holiday season. The song I remember most and associate with that time period is Dolly Parton's Hard Candy Christmas. Mother died January 9, 1987.

To this day I only have blotted out memories of how we all made it through that ordeal. She and I had shopped for her crypt and burial space at Woodlawn Cemetery together long beforehand. She wanted to be placed in the mausoleum there. She used to say that if anyone came to pay her respects after she was gone, she didn't want them to be out in the cold. She, herself, didn't want to be buried in the cold. The mausoleum would be more comfortable for all concerned.

Funeral services were held at the Church of the Madonna and were officiated by her good friend Reverend William Cunningham. I remember being there, and that the church was full of friends, family, and co-workers of both hers and mine. I remember being hugged and kissed and accepting offering of money that I turned over to Cunningham to use as he saw fit but in her name.

And then our lives moved on.

Michelle was enjoying her senior year of high school, I was finishing up a Bachelor Degree, and Dan was even doing better in elementary school. All of us would all end up graduating the following year in 1988. But still there was tension in the air.

Dan's mood would periodically darken and when I'd try to get him to tell me what was wrong it was if he couldn't. Eventually I just came out and asked him if he wanted to go live with his father and he said yes.

A Flip in the Script

I figured that after a week or two with Brian, Dan would come to his senses and want to come back home. But weeks grew into months and I was dismayed. Had I been wrong all this time? Had Brian changed? Was my son better off with his father?

Dan would bounce between Westbrook and Telegraph Rd seemingly at will. He always seemed happy and well cared for and Michelle and I were always glad to see him. But as Michelle got ready to head off to college, it hit me that I was still getting the short end of the stick. Once Dan started living with his father, Brian stopped paying any child support for him but I was still paying Dan's tuition. So this time, for the first time excluding the initial divorce proceedings, I filed a motion in court.

All I want, I told the judge, was for Brian to be required to pay Dan's tuition at the same school where he'd been attending until Dan either graduated or reached age eighteen, the same way I had done with his sister. And I wanted to be reimbursed for the tuition I had paid for Dan while Dan had been in his father's custody. Furthermore, I wanted the same visitation with Dan that Brian had previously been awarded by the courts. And I got it all.

Brian was mad. Apparently, whenever Dan's grades weren't quite satisfactory, Brian would drive him over to one of the worst high schools in the city and threaten to send Dan there if he didn't do better. And this terrified the boy.

I never knew what kind of arrangements Brian may have made with the Catholic school where I had paid my kid's tuition for years. What I do know is that no one from that institution ever reach out to support me in anyway despite my having served on their school board. There were times throughout the court proceedings when I felt I had gotten a cold shoulder from some of the officials there but I could never be sure. And other things were more important to me than pursuing their sudden, seeming dislike for me. I knew that Brian was in contact with them and, given his ability to charm almost anyone, it didn't surprise me one bit.

Apart for a couple of the teachers, the school seemed indifferent to me.

Once Michelle was happily ensconced at U of M, and after our house had been burglarized, I moved into a 2-bedroom apartment in a neighboring suburb. When Dan came to visit, he gradually began telling me horror stories about his relationship with his dad that included physical confrontations. I told Dan he could come back to live with me anytime he wanted, he just had to let me know. But the boy growing into his manhood felt he could handle it. It would be several weeks later before I'd get the call.

Can I come home, was all he said, and I answered back of course. I drove over to Westbrook and stayed parked in the driveway while Dan loaded up my car with his possessions. But just as he joined me in the vehicle, Brian pulled up behind me and blocked us in.

There was a standoff, a lot of back and forth arguing. Finally Dan went back into the house with his father and either agreed to stay there with him or was confined by him in some way. Eventually Brian came back out and backed up his car to let me out, and I drove home not knowing what else to do. Reluctantly, I called Katherine. I knew she had written off what I owed her, and

I was embarrassed seeking her advice, but I knew she would give it to me straight and she promptly verbalize what I already knew.

So I waited, and waited, until finally another call came.

Okay, said Dan, you can come get me. Just make sure the VCR is still in the car.

Huh?

Brian was willing to let Dan go as long as he could have the VCR back.

A done deal.

Over the next few years, the animosity lessened between Brian and me as I saw both our youngsters merge into adulthood.

Michelle would graduate with a double major from the University of Michigan four years after enrolling there, and then travel throughout Europe, and live and teach in Japan for two years before returning to the United States to forge her own career and marriage.

Dan would grow to recognize the multitude of layers that made up the person his father was, and would learn to latch on to some of them while discarding the rest. Eventually he'd relocate to Nashville to pursue his own songwriting career.

But before all of that, Brian developed cancer and it was Dan who not only nursed him through the latter stages of his life but also found him on his deathbed. Interestingly enough to me, before Brian died, he went back to England. I think it may have been to say his good byes. But in the end, he chose to come back to the United States, and Detroit in particular, to lay his head for the last time. He died August 11, 1998, three days before my birthday.

Judge Wahls also died that same year on November 24th. and also from cancer.

Since all of this, the years have flown too fast. And if there is one thing I've learned it that you can't let your past define you.

Life is a mixed bag, and you've just got to learn to live it the best you can.

Acknowledgement:

Special thanks to all thoses family members, friends and supporters, named and unnamed, who helped me over the years. Although we may have lost touch over time, your kindness and generosity will never be forgotten.

Made in the USA
Middletown, DE
21 April 2023

29052876R00073